JEREMY CADOC

SHOWDOWN IN JERICHO

A Novel

By

Reinhard Teichmann

Table of Contents

Chapter 1

Even though the young Reverend Jeremy Cadoc had not expected to be greeted with great fanfare by the town of Jericho, the reception he did get was even less of a welcome than he had imagined. The first bullet whistled past him almost before he heard the crack of the rifle and the second might have killed him had his mount not spooked and bolted up the main street of the town. As it was, the projectile creased his left arm, and he checked it, now that his horse had come to a stop in the protective shade of an oak tree. Only a flesh wound apparently; touching it with his right hand, he could feel the blood seeping through the material of his jacket, but there was nothing much he could do about it at the moment. First he had to get out of harms way. For the danger was not over. Who had been shooting at him and why?

Glancing up and down the sun-baked street, he could not detect any sign of his assailant. Nor was there any sign of any other living being. The clapboard structures with their false façades looked abandoned and there was not a sound to be heard anywhere, giving him the eerie feeling that he was in a ghost town. Where were all the inhabitants of Jericho – the shopkeepers, the farmers, ranchers and cowhands, the housewives and schoolchildren? Where were the horses and carriages that normally fill the streets of any thriving community? For that was how Jericho had been described to him – as a thriving community full of bustling activity, where a young minister like him, just out of the seminary, could make his mark and help build a growing parish.

Then a sound did reach his ears – some faint notes that were carried to him over a distance by the breeze, the voices of a choir singing a hymn. Of course! It was a Sunday, and they were all in church! That had to be the explanation! The eerie abandonment of the town was nothing more than a testimonial to the charisma of the minister currently in charge of this congregation, the fabled Reverend Macum Bersa, who held them all in his thrall. Jeremy had been assigned to him as an assistant. Sent by Methodist elders, he had travelled for weeks all the way from Dyersburg, Tennessee, in order to join this extraordinary man, to learn from him, to absorb his wisdom and become a pillar of the church, just like he was, and spurred on by the prospect of meeting the great figure so soon now, he turned his horse in the direction of the choir and made it canter up the empty street towards the top of the hill, where the white church structure was looming against the pale blue sky.

He was grateful that no one took further shots at him along the way for he didn't want his career to end even before he had consummated his still recent ordainment. However, when he got to the top, there was a reception committee waiting for him. Three brawny men dressed in black were blocking the entrance to the churchyard, gun belts flashing around their hips, two flanked the big door leading into the church itself, and still another sat in the bell tower, one leg dangling out, a shotgun propped up on his thigh. Rather than a house of the Lord this looked like a fortress, an unsettling sight for Jeremy. But the Reverend Bersa must have his reasons for the heavy protection, he thought. After all, this was pioneer country, full of unexpected perils – Indians and outlaws perhaps, and who knew what else. You couldn't expect things to be as civilized as back East.

Reminding himself of this, Jeremy dismounted, and after tying his horse to a hitching rail next to some other animals, approached the three men that guarded the gateway to the churchyard. "Howdy, gentlemen," he said, tipping his hat. "May I pass through?"

One of the men, who seemed to be their leader – tall and with a ruthless face – stepped forward and said, "And who are you?"

"Name's Cadoc, the Reverend Jeremy Cadoc," he said, tipping his hat and putting emphasis on the title, which he still wasn't quite used to, fresh out of the seminary as he was emerging. "I'm the new assistant," he added.

"The new assistant?"

"Yes, I'm here to serve under the Reverend Bersa. He's expecting me."

"He is? Well, he didn't say a word to us. Sorry, but we can't let you in."

"You got to let me through. Someone shot at me in town. I need help." He pointed at his injured arm, the drying blood glistening through the torn fabric of his jacket.

"Well, you'd better look somewhere else. Can't allow you to interrupt the service. Orders from the Reverend Bersa himself."

Jeremy was annoyed. "I don't understand. This is the house of the Lord. We all should be allowed access at any time."

"But not during the service." Murdoch said. He turned to the second man, a short, pork-bellied type with curly hair and a stubbly face. "Ain't that right, Higgins?"

"God's truth, Murdoch. The Reverend is mighty particular about that." He gave a short, cynical laugh and was joined in it by the third man, a skinny, sleazy looking individual who resembled a reptile.

"You tell him, Polk," Murdoch said to the reptile. "Tell him that's so."

"Yeah," Polk said, no longer smiling, and with a threatening undertone. "You'd better mosey on." Then he added bluntly, "Get lost."

Jeremy was shocked. What was going on here? First the ambush in town, now the rude and menacing rebuff. Something was deeply wrong here, and he didn't want to do their bidding without challenging them. The church was the house of the Lord and his rightful abode. Even if it was in the middle of the service, it wasn't correct that he should be kept from entering and from joining the congregation, which now had switched from singing to communal praying.

"I told you, Reverend Bersa is expecting me, " he said to Murdoch." He won't mind if I go in." He stepped around the tall man, intending to pass through the open gate, but was met there by yet another, younger man, also dressed in black, who had come up to observe the scene.

"Not so fast, my friend. You heard what my partners said. Get lost." The newcomer fixed his eyes sharply on Jeremy in order to emphasize his point.

If anything, it only served to fire up Jeremy more. "Who do you think you are?" he said. "You can't keep me from going in there. I came all the way across the country from Tennessee to serve in this community and now I'm finally here. I'm going in."

"Stop him, Curtin" Murdoch said. "Don't let him get past you."

But Jeremy would not let himself be discouraged. Not much older than Jeremy, Curtin was tall and muscular, but Jeremy's own physical assets were also considerable. Having grown up on a farm, and having participated in a generous amount of fist fighting as a boy, he concealed an impressive physique underneath his deceptive parson's attire, and this knowledge gave him confidence now. He would assert himself calmly and with the Lord's help would resolve the situation peacefully. And with a silent prayer on his lips, he approached the young tough who was blocking his way

"Please, brother, I ask you kindly, let me enter." When Curtin did not move and only shook his head, smiling condescendingly, Jeremy raised his hand to push him aside gently, but before he knew it, he found himself apprehended by two strong arms one moment, airborne the next, and finally stretched out on the unforgiving ground, having landed there with a violent crash.

"Ha, ha, ha…," the men guffawed, and they were joined by the two flanking the church and the one in the bell tower, all of whom had been watching the spectacle from some distance. "Ha, ha, ha". They kept it up for a while.

Stunned, Jeremy caught his breath, then gathered himself, brushed off the dust and picked up his hat. That had been rough treatment, which his instincts wouldn't allow him to go by unanswered, much as his Christian principles told him to do so. He had to stand up for himself. "Scum," it escaped from his lips.

That stopped their laughter. There was silence. The praying inside the church had now subsided, and you could have heard a pin drop. Higgins pretended to clear his ear with his little finger. "Did I hear right, Reverend. What you say?"

"Scum," Jeremy repeated more audibly.

"Well, now Reverend," Higgins said. " 'Tain't pleasing to the Lord to call decent folks names. 'Do unto your neighbor like you would do unto yourself' is what the holy book says, and cussing people don't go with that philosophy. I done gone to Sunday School myself when I was an itty baby, you know." He chuckled, and addressed the other men. "I think the Reverend needs to brush up on his scripture. What do you think, fellows, shall we teach him a lesson?"

"Sounds like a good idea," growled Murdoch. "A preacher who don't know the scripture is good for nothing. Polk, you want to do the honors?"

"I'd like nothing better," hissed the skinny man, and pulling a hunting knife from his boot, approached his victim. This young upstart, with his long, wavy dark-brown hair and burning dark eyes, who couldn't be more than twenty and was dressed like a greenhorn city slicker in a neat suit, shirt and tie, would be easy picking. He'd carve him up a little and complement that red stain on his arm with a few facial markings. It would make a pretty collage, a true work of art.

Jeremy stepped back as he saw Polk come towards him, and braced for the fight. The peaceful approach had not worked, and unfair as this contest would be, he had to deal with it as best he could, mustering all his survival skills. Of course, speaking about philosophy – yes, it did go against Jeremy's grain to be aggressive and violent, but in this case he had to make an exception. This was self-defense. This was not a question of turning the other cheek. It was clear that turning the other cheek would get him nowhere with these cynical ruffians. It literally could mean death for him, and what would that prove? Only that he perished even before he started on his noble career. Nobody would care that he had stood up for his principles, nor would the world actually ever learn about his heroics.

'Lord, forgive me and stand by me,' Jeremy prayed silently, steeling himself for Polk's attack as the latter came at him, flourishing his blade. Fortunately, knife fighting had also been part of Jeremy's rough-and-tumble country upbringing, and he now assumed an alert stance, bending forward, his arms and hands flexed like wings, ready to spring into action.

Polk seemed delighted. "Bring it on, Reverend," he beckoned. "Let's see what you've got." And then he lunged at him with the blade.

But Jeremy parried the blow, sweeping his arm aside before the knife could do any damage, and Polk, with some astonishment, retreated. Then he lunged again, and several more times Jeremy was able to avert his attack.

"Get him, Polk. Get him," Higgins egged him on, and Polk, whipped into a rage, at last found his mark. Jeremy had not been quick enough, and the blade nicked him on the chin. A few more parried blows, then another cut, on the cheek this time. Then a slice on his forehead, causing blood to flood Jeremy's left eye - a dangerous development. They had been dancing in a circle, Jeremy trying to find an opportunity to grab Polk between lunges in order to wrestle him down, but this approach had not been fruitful. Polk was too quick and elusive, skinny and light on his feet as he was, floating sideways, backward and forward swiftly, indeed like a scurrying lizard. A different, more proactive approach was necessary.

They had paused to catch their breaths, and Jeremy wiped the blood off his face. Polk was eyeing him with a crazed, entranced expression. "Look at him, ain't the Reverend pretty?" he called out to the others, who looked on from the sidelines. "My best piece of work yet."

"Yes, a masterpiece," Murdoch said sarcastically. "You're a real virtuoso. Now finish him off."

"Yeah, finish him off!" Higgins screeched excitedly. "Get the bastard!"

It was enough to make Jeremy dig deeper into his repertoire of fighting moves. When Polk, with a howl, lunged at him again, this time clearly going for the death blow, Jeremy, energized by a new surge of adrenalin, deftly grabbed his wrist and with his free hand pushed back Polk's head, piercing his eyes with two fingers, an action which brought another howl from Polk's lips – this time of pain. A moment later Jeremy was standing behind him, choking him, and having grabbed the knife from Polk, was holding it to the man's throat, pressing the sharp blade lightly into the skin, while with his other hand he twisted one of Polk's arms upward behind the man's back.

Murdoch and Higgins, and all the others who had witnessed the fight, were stunned. All of it had happened so quickly that they had no time to react. Murdoch made a tentative move to pull out his Colt, and so did Higgins, but Jeremy warned them, "No gunplay gentlemen. Throw your weapons down."

They hesitated.

"I mean it. Throw them down." He dug the blade a little deeper into Polk's throat and gave an extra twist to the arm behind his back, making the man groan. "I'm going to kill him if I have to," he said, and Murdoch and Higgins obeyed, pulling their guns out of their holsters and dropping them, and so did Curtin.

"Now get out my way. We're going in."

"You won't get away with this, Preacher," Murdoch said as Jeremy brushed past him.

Jeremy paid no attention to him. Instead he fixed his gaze on the church, as he pushed Polk forward into the yard and down the path towards the large white structure, all the while pressing the hunting blade against Polk's throat. As their little procession arrived at the big wooden door, the two men guarding it stepped aside without reaching for their six shooters. Nor did the man in the bell tower make any motions to use his long-barreled gun.

They all seemed transfixed by the spectacle unfolding before their eyes.

"Open the door," Jeremy bellowed. "And open both wings wide. Get a move on or I'll slash his throat."

The two door guards didn't need to be asked twice. They quickly stepped up to unbolt the big, arched portal, and pulling hard, unfolded the two heavy leaves all the way, revealing a cavernous interior, from which the sound of many singing voices poured forth -- for the congregation had started another hymn.

"Amazing grace how sweet the sound…," the harmonies of the familiar melody welled up, and it strengthened Jeremy's resolve. With the Lord by his side, he could face any adversity. Nothing could go wrong.

"Move," he ordered, pushing Polk ahead.

And this was how the young Reverend Jeremy Cadoc, recent graduate of the Methodist seminary in Dyersburg, Tennessee, first presented himself to his new congregation and to his new pastor.

Chapter 2

The Reverend Macum Bersa was indeed an extraordinary man. Nearly seven feet tall, with a massive frame and a huge, square head that was fringed by a mess of long red locks and a thick crimson mustache and beard, he looked like a fairytale giant ready to devour any disobedient human who got in his way. Standing on the dais in front of the altar, and leading the congregation with his booming voice, he was a truly imposing presence, and Jeremy did not know whether to feel intimidated or heartened as he pushed the stumbling Polk ahead of him down the center aisle. He chose the latter. Surely the Reverend had been advised of Jeremy's arrival, and surely he would receive him with open arms.

As he and Polk advanced and as the congregation in the pews on both sides became more and more aware of them, the singing started to ebb, and by the time he and Polk arrived at the altar, it stopped altogether, including Reverend Bersa's voice, whose absence left a big void. There was a long, drawn-out moment of silence. Then it was Bersa who spoke.

"What, in the Lord's name, is the meaning of this? Who are you?" his voice boomed, echoing through the building and making the walls tremble.

"I'm Jeremy Cadoc, the new assistant," Jeremy said. "I just arrived in town. This man and his friends gave me a reception I didn't deserve, as you can see. They wouldn't let me come in. They said those were your orders."

"They were my orders," Bersa said. "But they were meant for others….you can let the man go," he added. "You're safe now."

There were more armed men in black lined up against the wall, and Bersa motioned to one of them, and when he approached, Jeremy released Polk into his custody. Then Bersa addressed the still stunned and confused congregation – men, women and children in their Sunday best who listened to him with rapt attention. "Due to unforeseen circumstances we'll have to cut our service short today. God bless you all, and we see each other next Sunday. May the Lord be with you. " He made a big sign of the cross over them, and as they got up and turned to leave, he said to Jeremy, "I've been expecting you, young man. Let's go to the parish house, where we can patch you up."

They left through a side door, where a horse-drawn coach was waiting for them, an unexpected touch of luxury for a preacher. Weren't men of the Lord supposed to be humble and use more basic means of transportation? But once they were inside the vehicle and rolling, Jeremy couldn't help but sink into the comfort of the plush upholstery, exhausted as he was from the ordeal of his arrival. Bersa, sitting opposite him, pulled out a cigar from an inside pocket of his elegant silk suit, which he lit nonchalantly, tossing the match out the coach window. More touches of luxury that were not germane to a preacher's lifestyle, Jeremy thought. Bare-threaded, ill-fitting attire was more the rule for clergymen, and that they smoked cigars was totally out-of–character.

Bersa had a few puffs and he must have noticed the astonishment in Jeremy's face, for he said, "You're surprised that I smoke, Reverend? It's a habit I've acquired here in Jericho. Life is hard out here on the frontier, and few are the comforts, and this is one that makes things bearable."

"I understand," Jeremy said politely, though in all truth he could not quite fathom Bersa's rationale. But he guessed he had to get used to the way things were handled in this new environment.

"Let me first of all apologize for the inhospitable treatment my men gave you today," Bersa continued, taking another puff. "It was a case of mistaken identity. Yes, we had been expecting you, but not so soon. The message I received from Dyersburg said you wouldn't arrive until next month. My men thought you were someone else – an impostor. We've had quite a few impostors come through here and make trouble – impostors, thieves, killers and marauders -- and we're having to take extraordinary measures to protect ourselves."

Jeremy nodded. "Of course." It sounded exaggerated, but out of politeness he did not question Bersa's explanation.

"That's why I formed this corps of guards," the big man went on, "all of them very capable with a gun – to keep the parish safe and allow us to dedicate ourselves to the Lord's work peacefully. The Crusaders I've called them. They fight for the Lord. They fight for Jericho."

As the coach rolled on, Jeremy could see several of the black-clad guards through the window accompanying them on their horses, among them Murdoch and Polk, and for all of Bersa's explanations he did not feel very reassured. These men did not look pious and God fearing, and he knew from his personal experience that they weren't. But again he did not want to ruffle any feathers and kept quiet. Then another matter popped into his head. "May I ask what happened to McLoughlin?" McLoughlin was the assistant who had preceded him and whom he had been sent to replace. The elders in Dyersburg had told him to inquire about him because they had not heard from him.

"McLoughlin?" Bersa's expression turned from animated to somber. "I'm afraid, McLoughlin passed away. An accident, you see. Fell off a horse and broke his neck. And a fine lad he was. We gave him a fine funeral. The whole town attended. We all miss him a lot." He seemed almost moved to tears, and in fact wiped some moisture, real or imaginary, from under his eye.

Jeremy, too, was moved. He had never met the last assistant personally, but out of solidarity with a brother-in-arms, he felt a deep sympathy. "I'm sorry to hear that. I want to visit his grave as soon as I get a chance, and say a prayer for his soul."

"You do that," Bersa said, taking another puff from his cigar. They had reached their destination in the center of town, and the carriage stopped. "We have arrived, Reverend."

One of the Crusaders opened the coach door and Bersa climbed out. When Jeremy came out after him, he found a surprise waiting for him..

"This," Bersa proclaimed with a flourish," is our parish house."

Jeremy's jaw dropped. If he had expected a sober, modest structure, he was mistaken. This was an expansive two-storey building with a fancy façade, a swing door and a garish sign proclaiming THE PARADISE.

"But this is the saloon," he exclaimed.

"You're right," Bersa agreed. "We had to transfer our church quarters here after the original ones burned down. This was the only place in town with the capacity to accommodate us – our offices, plus my living quarters, and by the way, quarters for you as well. As soon as we get the funds, we'll build something else."

Jeremy somehow doubted that, but he had to play along with the preacher. Taking him by the elbow, Bersa said, "Let's go in, Reverend, so you can get to know the place and we can take care of you." They passed through the swing door, and a honky-tonk piano greeted them, its happy notes providing entertainment for those who sat around several round tables, playing cards and drinking hard liquor – men in black who must have come here even before the church service had ended, and loose women who kept them company. Jeremy was appalled. If this building served as the church's headquarters, how could Bersa allow these sinful saloon activities to continue? Increasingly concerned, he followed the big preacher as they made their way through the noisy crowd, some of whom raised their glasses for a toast, others intoning "Glory, Glory Hallelujah….." as if to mock Jeremy. Out of the corner of his eyes he noticed the paunchy Higgins and the reptile Polk, as well as the youth who had manhandled him, Curtin, and feeling highly uncomfortable, he was only too happy when Bersa led him up a winding staircase to the second floor, where he opened a door off a hallway, "Welcome, Reverend. These are my chambers. Won't you come in?"

"Thank you, " Jeremey said, grateful when Bersa closed the door and the din subsided. "Your men are rough and they play hard."

"Just letting off a little steam on a Sunday. Doing the Lord's work is stressful, and they deserve an opportunity to relax. They'll be all the much better for it come Monday morning."

Jeremy found that hard to believe, nor could he quite digest the décor of the room they found themselves in: red velvet curtains, gold-leaf patterned wallpaper, a satin covered canopy bed, a gilded chandelier and gold framed paintings all the way around – dazzling opulence everywhere. Would the surprises ever end? Apparently not, for Bersa now asked him, "Can I offer you a drink, Reverend? He walked to a table with several bottles and glasses. "Bourbon? Scotch? What's your fancy?"

"Nothing, thank you. I don't drink."

Bersa poured himself a glass, and having noticed Jeremy's shock, explained with an ironic smile, "Another one of the comforts of frontier life, Reverend. Sooner or later you'll develop your own." He pointed to a plush Otoman, ""Please, take a seat. In a minute we'll get you fixed up." He took off his jacket and with drink in hand, leaned back on the canopy bed, which was large enough to accommodate his outsized frame. He took a sip and placed his glass on a side table. Then he clapped his hands.

Seemingly out of nowhere a female appeared – a shapely brunette dressed in black lace lingerie, which displayed her assets seductively. "Macum, baby," she exclaimed. "I've missed you so much."

"Not as much as I've missed you, Brandy. Come to daddy." He opened his arms wide, and she ran up to the bed and threw herself into them, whereupon they engaged in a very sensual welcome.

Yet another one of Bersa's choice frontier comforts, Jeremy thought, as he was watching in awe and disgust from his vantage point on the Otoman . Could anything top this? Was there still more to come? Nonetheless, he decided to keep his feelings to himself, based on the reasoning that he had just barely arrived. There would be a better time and a better place.

Bersa now disengaged himself from his mistress, pushing her away. "Hold on, honey. We have a guest," he said, motioning in Jeremy's direction. "We shouldn't be impolite. May I present to you the Reverend Jeremy Cadoc, our new assistant."

"Pleased to meet you."

"And this is Brandy, my fiancé"

"A pleasure."

Jeremy doubted that they were really engaged. He thought that Bersa was using the label just as a cover. Brandy didn't look like the marrying type.

"What happened to Reverend Cadoc's face?" Brandy asked.

"An accident on the road," Bersa said. "Go get some gauze and ointment to fix him up."

She disappeared through a side door that blended seamlessly into the wall and presently returned with the items, and approaching Jeremy, asked, "May I clean your face?"

He nodded, and she took a few minutes to dab his wounds and apply the cream, Jeremy wincing a little now and then. When she was finished, she turned to Bersa, "How does he look?"

"A lot better," Bersa pronounced. "And now, can you bring us some food, honey? The Reverend must be starved."

"Right away, Macum." And once more she left.

Bersa got up from the bed and pulled up a chair to join Jeremy, "Well now, Reverend Cadoc, there are still a few further matters that I need to discuss with you – matters that need to be kept private and just between you and me."

"Oh? What matters?"

"Administrative matters. Financial matters. You see this parish is underfunded. The Diocese in Tennessee is not helping us any, and we have to rely on our own devices. In order to be able to continue the Lord's work I have instituted a system where the parishioners contribute set amounts of money on a regular basis, but this system hinges on reliability. We need to be able to count on that income. I have the Crusaders to help me achieve that, but I need your cooperation as well, Reverend Cadoc."

"What exactly are you referring to, Reverend Bersa?"

"Money, my friend, plain and simple. There's lots to be made in this town, and between you and me we can get rich. See all this…" he made a gesture around the room. "You can have it all – wine, women and song, if you just play along with me. So what do you say?"

Brandy stepped in with a tray of hors d'oeuvres that she placed in front of Jeremy on a small table. "Here you are Reverend. Enjoy"

But Jeremy had lost his appetite and paid no attention to the food. Had he heard correctly? Was Bersa proposing that he should participate in an illicit conspiracy of corruption? Was he callously bilking all these honest parishioners, and did he expect Jeremy to help him in this? No wonder the man could afford all these luxuries.

Outraged, Jeremy was about to tell him off when Bersa ratcheted up the offer another notch. "I'll even throw in this little filly," he said, grabbing Brandy by the hand. "Come here baby, show the Reverend a good time." He pushed her in Jeremy's direction and she slid into the Otoman next to him, nestling up to him, unbuttoning his jacket and shirt and nuzzling his chest. Although the sensation was not unpleasant, Jeremy at last reacted, pushing her off himself onto the floor. He jumped to his feet. Enough was enough. Having observed polite etiquette to the utmost, he decided the time had come to give Bersa a piece of his mind, for better or worse. "Look here," he said, and the adrenaline gave him the courage to grab the big man's shirt and pull his face close to his own. "I get it now. You're a corrupt old bastard, and you want me to be your partner in crime. Well, sorry but I can't oblige. Fact is, I'm gonna head straight back for Tennesse in the morning to inform the elders. This can't be tolerated." He let go of Bersa, who was visibly shaken, but recovered in an instant.

"No, you're not," he said, smoothing his shirt.
"What?"

"You're not going back to Tennessee in the morning," Bersa said, and before Jeremy could retort anything, he called to the door, "Guard, take this man away."

The door opened, and who else but the paunchy Higgins sauntered in, a smug smile on his stubbly face.

"Lock him up safely," Bersa said. "Make sure he doesn't get away."

"I'll take care of him, boss. Don't you worry none." Higgins pulled his gun and held it at Jeremy. "Nice to see you again, Reverend. Come with me. And don't make any wrong moves."

With his gun, Higgins pointed to the door, and Jeremy had no other option but to walk ahead of him as they left the room.

+   +   +

When Jeremy opened his eyes, he was at first disoriented. His head hurt badly, and he found himself lying on the floor in the dark. Where was he and what had happened? Then it all came back. Higgins had taken him down a long hallway to a back room, into which he had shoved him with the words, "Sleep well, Reverend," raising his pistol and bringing it down on Jeremy's skull with a crash. How long he had been out he didn't know, but it must have been for quite a while for the sun had gone down and the room was engulfed in shadows.

His first thought was escape, and getting on his feet, he approached a small square window through which filtered some pale rays of moonlight. But when he tried to force it open, he found that it was firmly secured. Even if he could have succeeded, it wouldn't have helped him any, for the drop to the ground was very steep and there were two black-clad guards lingering behind the saloon by some horses. It would have been impossible to get past them without being noticed. He decided to try the door, but was stopped in his tracks by voices.

"Howdy Hig, ready for your break?" It was Curtin, the young thug who had manhandled him at the church-yard upon his arrival.

"Sure am. I'm bored to death sitting here all this time."

"How's that punk Reverend doing?"

"He's okay. I checked on him a while ago, and he was still out. He ain't gonna give you no trouble."

"Well, he's got spunk, I'll give him that," Curtin continued. "Miller tried to bring him down with a couple of bullets when he arrived in town and he got away.
Then Cadoc bested Polk at the church-yard. And he even had the balls to stand up to Bersa, can you believe it? I wonder what the old man is gonna do to him now."

"That don't take much guessing…"

"What do you mean, Hig?"

"I'm saying he'll do the same to him as he did to the other one – McLoughlin."

"What, another accident?"

"That's right, Curtin. He'll fall off a horse, and that's it. Case closed."

"Yeah, and there'll be a nice funeral, and we'll all have a great time."

They both laughed heartily, and Jeremy had an urge to open the door and punish them for their cynicism, but he knew it was wiser to control himself. It would have been self-defeating. But having overheard the conversation of the two guards, everything became clear now. His predecessor, McLoughlin, had gone through a similar ordeal as himself, and for not cooperating with Bersa, had paid with his life. And now the same fate was waiting in store for Jeremy. He couldn't let this happen. He had to do something. As Higgins was taking leave from Curtin and he heard the latter settle down on a chair outside the door, he said a silent prayer, as all humans do in desperate situations, including disbelievers, 'Please, God, help me out of this. I'll be grateful to you forever. I'll commend myself into your hands."

And the miracle happened. Out of nowhere a shadow materialized, ghost-like in the pale moonlight, wearing a cape and floating through the room towards him – Bersa's mistress, Brandy, he realized when he took a closer look. "Where did you come from?" he asked in amazement.

"Shshsh," she placed her finger on her lips. "Come with me, Reverend," she whispered, grabbing his hand. "We have no time to lose."

Without questioning her any further, Jeremy followed her out a nearly invisible side door, similar to the one in Bersa's room, then down a secondary hallway that was drowned in darkness. They passed several other doors, presumably guest rooms in back of the saloon, then came to one from which suggestive sounds issued. Brandy stopped. "Shshsh," she said one more time.

"What's going on?" Jeremy whispered.

She pointed to the door, and he took a peek through a crack from which poured a sliver of light. And what he saw very nearly floored him: a torture room with whips, chains and other instruments hanging on the walls, with Bersa, the big man, in the center, strapped to a rack, face down, in all his naked glory, one of the scantily clad saloon girls lashing his buttocks with crop.

"Hit me," Bersa exclaimed as his body convulsed. "Hit me, Charysse, hit me, hit me – yes, yes, yes, yes…" Finally he shuddered to a halt, the girl unstrapped him and after catching his breath, he turned over on what was really a soft matress. "By God, that was good for the soul. Thank you Lord," he said and beckoned to his sexy torturer, a blond bombshell of a female, "Come here, honey, give me some more of your sweet loving."

Jeremy turned away. "Disgusting," he whispered under his breath. Yes, what he had witnessed was repulsive and outrageous! Here was the ultimate proof of Bersa's depravity. The man was corrupt to the core in every way, morally and spiritually, in addition to his sexual perversion, and all of it was carried out under the mantel of hypocritical piety and godliness. Could there be a greater sacrilege than the words Bersa had just uttered? With fury welling up inside him once more, Jeremy felt like barging in there and breaking up the gross scene, but he was held back by the sight of a couple of black-clad guards standing in the shadows of the torture room, who would have made any intervention futile. There would come a day of reckoning for Bersa in the future, he swore to himself. But it had to be postponed for now.

Brandy pulled him away. "Let's get out of here."

They continued to the end of the hallway and down some stairs, stopping at an exit that led to the yard behind the Paradise. The two Crusaders he had seen from the window above were still lingering next to the horses.

"Try to make a run for it," Brandy said. "Go to the Harrison place on the road out of town, just about a mile past the church. You can't miss it. My parents, Will and Lena, are there, and so is my brother, Chuck. Tell them I sent you. They'll take care of you."

Jeremy nodded. "I don't know how to thank you. Why are you doing all this for me?"

"I have my reasons," she said. "I'll tell you some other time. " She bent forward, kissing him on the cheek, "Good luck, Reverend."

His skin burning from the unexpected touch of her lips, he opened the door by a crack to survey the situation. The two guards were leaning against a hitching rail, talking in low tones, their backs turned towards him, their horses tied on next to them. Much as his peaceful nature rebelled against it, he needed to find a strong way to handle them – friendly persuasion was out of the question. The only thing left was to pull a bluff, and it had to be a very daring one. He would sneak up behind them, he decided, and threaten them, pretending he had a weapon. As so many times already, he would place himself in the Lord's hands, trusting he would help him through this. And doing so, he opened the door a little wider and slipped out into the dark.

Ducking low, he succeeded in sneaking up on the men without alerting them. Absorbed in their conversation, the two had not paid attention to what was going on behind their backs, and when they now heard Jeremy's sharp voice ringing out behind them, they were startled indeed. "Raise them up, fellows."

They instantly stopped talking, then, hesitantly began to obey the command.

"Faster. And don't turn around."

Again they obeyed. "What the hell….," one of them started. But Jeremy cut him off. "Shut up."

The men stood still like statues, their hands up high in the air. Amazed that his ploy had actually worked, Jeremy decided to relieve them of their six shooters and proceeded to pull the weapons out of their holsters one after the other from behind. He tossed one of the guns aside and kept the other, training it on the two guards as he now stepped around to face them.

"Don't try anything " he said as he untied the two horses, and slapping one of them on the haunch, sent it galloping off into the night. Still training the gun in his hand on the two Crusaders, he got on the second horse. "Give my regards to Bersa,," he said and was about to give his mount the heels, but the Crusader who had talked up before yelled out, "I ain't gonna let you get away with it, Preacher." Reaching down to his boot, he pulled out a derringer and pointed it at Jeremy. But before he could squeeze the trigger, Jeremy fired the weapon in his own hand and the man collapsed. Spooked by the explosion, Jeremy's horse charged forward into the night, Jeremy's mind reeling. For the first time in his life he had used a gun! He had killed his first man!

Chapter 3

Jeremy did not have time to reflect on the enormity of these events as he was racing through the pitch-black darkness. He was too busy finding his way to the Harrisons' property. Having passed the church, he left Jericho's last houses behind and passed a ranch or two and finally arrived at an isolated homestead that he thought belonged to Brandy's folks. A dog started barking as he drew closer, and a door opened, light pouring out. A man stepped into the frame, shotgun in one hand and an oil lamp in the other. "Roble, stay back," he said, then asking, "Who goes?"

Jeremy got off his horse, almost falling down in the process, and the other man steadied him. "And who are you?"

"I'm Cadoc, Reverend Jeremy Cadoc. Is this the Harrison place?"

"Yes. I'm Chuck."

Jeremy could not help noticing that he resembled Brandy a lot – the same dark-brown hair, the same chiseled features; only he looked a few years older, somewhere around thirty. "Your sister sent me here. She said you could help me."

"You surely look like you could use some help, Reverend. You're all beaten up. What happened?"

"That's a long story."

"Well, come inside, and meet my folks."

The house was simple and made of logs, with a cooking area in one part and a living area in another. At a table in the center there sat two spare, silvery-haired figures, Will and Lena presumably. Chuck introduced Jeremy, mentioning Brandy. When they heard her name, the two seniors became visibly animated, and Will asked, "How is she doing? We haven´t seen her in months."

"My little baby," Lena cried out. "Is she all right?"

Jeremy sank onto a chair. "Yes, she is. I saw her at the Paradise and she looked fine – at least in body if not in spirit. She helped me escape from the place and from Bersa." And then he told them briefly what had happened to him earlier that day at the saloon. Lena brought him some soup, and as he started to eat it, he almost collapsed from exhaustion. After only a few bites, he had to stop.

"You'd better get some rest," Chuck said. "You look like you need it. Tomorrow we talk more."

Lena took him to a back room, where he fell asleep on a makeshift bed, worn out from the events of the day – the most dramatic day of his life – and he did not wake up until late next morning.

+   +   +

Over breakfast they told him about Brandy, and it cleared up a lot of things for him. They related to him how Bersa pressed all the young girls of the town into service at the Paradise, and how Brandy had become his chosen mistress, never allowed to leave the saloon premises. "He exploits all the young girls and keeps them in line with the help of the Crusaders," Chuck explained. "Any problem with any of them and he sends the guards to their homes to intimidate their families. And he does the same with the townsfolk. He levies an outrageous tithe, and when they refuse to pay, he moves in with the Crusaders, taking their property and killing them if he has to."

Jeremy listened to their heart wrenching complaints attentively, and now he understood what Brandy had not had the time to tell him when she helped him escape from the Paradise. Deeply moved, he said, "Something must be done about it. Has anyone ever tried?"

"As a matter of fact, yes," said Chuck.

"Who?"

"The last parochial assistant, McLoughlin."

So what Jeremy had suspected was true. "What happened?"

"McLoughlin tried to organize the town to take a stand against Bersa. But it didn't work. Bersa found out about it and had him killed – supposedly a fall from a horse, but we all know what really happened."

Jeremy nodded. "Well, you can't give up. You have to try again. If you give up,you'll be finished. You'll be kissing Bersa's feet forever."

"We know that," Chuck said. "But we need a leader. There is no one in Jericho left who has the courage to stand up to Bersa, after all that happened. We need someone who can unite all the citizens and instill faith in them – enough faith to overcome this evil force, this Satan. We need someone," he hesitated, and his eyes lit up with a sudden inspiration, "someone like you, Reverend. Yes , someone like you."

Overwhelmed by the trust Chuck placed in him, Jeremy did not know what to say. To lead a rebellion against Bersa, the fabled minister in charge of this parish, had been the farthest thing on his mind, especially having just arrived in town. The most he had been planning to do was to return to Tennessee and inform the Diocese of what was going on here so that they could take the appropriate measures. Chuck's suggestion came upon him a bit fast. "Let me think about it," he said.

They were interrupted by a banging on the door, which brought Roble to his feet, making his hackles rise and causing him to bark fiercely.

"Open up, Harrison. We need to check your house."

"Be right there," Chuck called out. He turned to Jeremy, "The Crusaders. They must be looking for you. We got to get you out of here. Follow my Pa."

"Come with me," Will said and getting up with unsuspected energy let him out a back door, directing him to the barn, where Jeremy found a loft to hide in. From there he tried to piece together what was going on at the main house, based on the loud voices he was hearing. There was a lot of shouting by the Crusaders who had arrived, and more subdued answers by Chuck. Then the voices subsided, indicating that they must have gone into the house. Finally the voices got louder again and came closer. They were coming to the stable. Jeremy had better be alert. He had already pulled the ladder up into the loft so it wouldn't arouse suspicions, but anything could happen if they checked here.

Fortunately the danger passed quickly, though there was one tense moment. As they were stepping around the barn underneath, looking for Jeremy in different corners, including the horse pens, one of the Crusaders said, "Hey, look what I found"

"What?" asked his partner.

"This roan. It looks like mine."

"Really?"

"Yeah, the one the Preacher ran off with."

"Are you sure?"

"Sure I'm sure. It's got the same white marking on its face. I swear it does."

Chuck interceded. "That's a stray. I found it outside the house last night standing in the dark. My dog alerted me."

"Well, I'll be damned," said the Crusader, who claimed to be the animal's owner. "And you're still saying that Preacher ain't around?"

"That's right," Chuck insisted. "The horse was alone."

"That sounds mighty suspicious to me."

"That's exactly how it happened. The animal just arrived, and there was no rider."

The Crusader seemed to hesitate. "Okay, we'll take your word for it, Harrison. We've just about looked in every corner of this place. But if it turns out you're lying, you're going to be in trouble, I tell you – in deep trouble. You understand?"

"I understand. But I'm not lying."

"Well, you'd better not," the horse's owner emphasized. "Meantime, I'm gonna take that filly with me. Let's get out of here."

"Let's go," said his partner.

Jeremy heard them all leave the barn and waited until Chuck came back when the coast was clear. Only then did he put the ladder back where it had been and climbed to the ground.

"That was close, Reverend," Chuck said

"Yes, it was. I just hope they won't come back."

"Let's hope not."

They went back to the main house and informed Will and Lena of what had happened. The two old timers were still shaking, and hearing about the events in the stable only added to their anxiety. Chuck told them to calm down, assuring them that they were safe, that the Crusaders had accepted his explanation, which had been logical enough. There was no reason for them to return. And they finally did relax and go back to their normal activities around the house, Lena cooking in the kitchen and Will getting firewood from out back.

Chuck and Jeremy sat at the table and had a cup of coffee. "You see how people feel around here?" Chuck resumed the conversation from earlier in the morning. "They're scared to the bone. My folks are a good example."

"I can see that," Jeremy said.

"Things are getting worse in town," Chuck continued. "No one's coming to help us – not the church and not the law. We sent for a Marshall and got no response, and the only response we got from the Methodist diocese was for them to send you. You're our only hope, Reverend."

Yes, but apparently the church elders hadn't sent him to police Macum Bersa and clean up corruption. They had not mentioned a word about any of this to him, but this was reality and he had to deal with it. He could not run from it. These people needed help, and it was his duty as a man of God to provide that help. Coming to a decision, he said, "If I do it, I need the whole town to be on my side. Everybody will need to work together. That's the only way we can get it done."

"Of course, Reverend. I'll give you all the help I can to get them organized."

"Good. And then there is another thing."

"What?"

"My personal safety. I want to learn how to use a gun. I don't want to happen to me what happened to McLoughlin."

"That's no problem, Reverend. I can teach you."

"Chuck is a great marksman," Lena said, pouring them some more coffee. "He got first prize in the local shooting contest last year." She smiled proudly.

"Okay. When do we get started?"

"Tomorrow," Chuck said. "After you get another day of rest. Some more rest will do you good."

+   +   +

The next morning they rode out to the canyons on the two horses that were left in the Harrison's stable. And there they practiced, Jeremy using the Colt that he had taken from the Crusader the night he had escaped from the Paradise. Feeling the weapon in his hand again, he was reminded of that moment – that fateful moment that he had shot the man who had pulled the derringer on him. It had only taken a split second, his finger squeezing the trigger automatically, as if in a trance, in response to the threat, and yet, it had also been somehow empowering. For that one moment he felt in control of his fate, under the most adverse circumstances. Yes, he had killed, that was true, but it was in self-defense, and if he had to do it again, it would only be for a noble purpose. But to try to cleanse the town from sin without a gun was out of the question. It would end in defeat.

And so he honed his shooting skills, day after day, Chuck setting up targets – bottles and cans, and after he ran out of them, rocks and pieces of wood. Chuck had given Jeremy a gun belt and holster and taught him how to draw smoothly and quickly, how to aim with precision and make sure he hit his target with consistency, increasing the difficulty level as Jeremy got better, tossing multiple objects in the air at once which Jeremy had to pulverize. This Jeremy did with great enthusiasm, improving his skill day by day. After four weeks had gone by, one day after practice, Chuck said, "You're a great shot now, Reverend. You'd beat even me in any contest. There's nothing more I can teach you."

"Thanks, Chuck. I guess I'm ready now." The urgency to act had been building up in him for a while, as he had regained his strength fully and his bruised body, along with his face, had healed. Yes, he was ready for Bersa. "Let's go into town to see the Sheriff. He can help us get everyone together."

"That's right, Reverend. If anyone can get it done, it'll be him."

"Then, let's go tonight."

"Okay."

They went back to the Harrison home and waited for nightfall, and then, with Will and Lena's blessings, set out for the town. But before Jeremy was ready to set in motion his rescue plan for Jericho, there was one other mission he wanted to carry out..

+   +   +

Boothill looked forlorn in the dusk as Jeremy and Chuck pulled up outside its walls and dismounted. Leaving their horses at the gate, they entered the locale in order to look for a certain grave among the many that were scattered about the bare patch of desert. Most of them were marked with a simple wooden cross that had a name inscribed; otherwise there was not much else to distinguish one from the other. Chuck took the lead in examining them one by one, moving around different parts of the graveyard, until he finally cried out, "Here it is, Reverend."

Jeremy rushed up to where he stood. Yes, it was his predecessor's tomb all right. 'Reverend Joshua McLoughlin,' the sign read in uneven, scrawled letters, and underneath the name, in small characters, was legible the still recent date of his demise. The grave was so new that the mound that had been heaped over the casket had not receded into the ground yet. Jeremy was saddened. "Let us pray," he said, taking his hat off, and Chuck did the same. "Lord," he began. "I ask you to give me the strength to overcome evil in this town and get justice for this poor soul that died on your behalf. He did not deserve this fate. I pray for his soul. I commend myself and my partner, Chuck, into your hands. Please, be with us, oh Lord! Amen."

"Amen," said Chuck.

Just as they were finishing, there was a shuffle behind them, accompanied by a snarling voice, "Well, if it ain't the preacher…." Spinning around, Jeremy and Chuck reached for their guns, but it was too late. They were staring down the barrels of two Colts pointed at them by two men dressed in black barely distinguishable in the dark – Crusaders clearly.

"Drop your weapons," the one who had done the talking, ordered. And Jeremy and Chuck had no other recourse but to obey. "What are you two doing out here anyway?"

"Saying goodbye to a friend," Jeremy said.

"A friend? Ah, I get it – the other punk of a preacher that was gonna be the boss' helper, the one we buried here. A troublemaker just like you, but not as tough. Didn't put up any kind of fight, not even when his life was on the line. Not a peep when I snapped his neck – snapped it just like a chicken bone." He laughed derisively.

Jeremy was furious. "You broke his neck? I thought he fell off a horse."

"Not a chance. The Reverend Bersa wanted to get rid of him fast, so he didn't want to waste the time staging an accident. He had me take care of the matter. I do say I did a very professional job."

"Bastard," Jeremy cried out and moved to throw himself on the speaker, but the other simply raised his gun up higher.

"Easy now, Reverend," he said coldly. "Or I'll let you have it right here. Mind you, my boss wants you alive. He made us look all over for you. He'll be very happy when we bring you in."

"And who do we have here? The Harrison boy, if I'm not wrong," said the other Crusader. "The boss will be mighty glad that we bring him in too."

"That's right. Now you tie them up, Jackson while I keep my gun on them."

"Hold out your hands," Jackson said to Jeremy and Chuck as he holstered his gun, pulled out a knife and sliced two lengths of rope off a lasso.

Jeremy knew that this was his only chance. If he did not act now, their whole effort would be over before it had even begun. Organizing the town, overcoming Bersa, re-establishing justice and bringing back civilization to Jericho – none of that would ever be realized if he let this moment slip by unused. Already Jackson had tied up Chuck and now it was Jeremy's turn. When Jackson started to sling the rope around his forearms, Jeremy decided to make his move, and swinging up his arms, knocked the man in his face hard, stunning him. As he had done with Polk at the church-yard, Jeremy managed to twirl the man around, keeping him in front of himself as a shield, simultaneously pulling the man's gun out of his holster and pointing it at the man's temple.

"Drop your gun," Jeremy ordered the other Crusader.

The man, who stood about fifteen feet away, did not react immediately, standing as if paralyzed.

"Drop the gun," Jeremy repeated. "Or Jackson will get it."

"Don't let him kill me," Jackson groaned, writhing under Jeremy's grip. Then there was a shot and Jackson slumped. A bullet fired by Jackson's partner and meant for Jeremy had found Jackson's chest accidentally. And now came more bullets meant for Jeremy but impacting Jackson, and Jeremy himself started firing the weapon in his own hand, aiming at the other Crusader – a full-fledged gun battle ensuing. Jeremy advanced at his opponent until he was almost close to the touch, all the while using Jackson, who was lifeless by now, as a shield. Then the gunfire stopped abruptly and Jackson's partner was lying lifeless on the ground. Jeremy dropped the cadaver in his arm that had been his salvation. He touched each of the two bodies on the ground with his boot.

"They're both gone," he said, turning around to Chuck behind him. "Didn't mean for them to die, but there was no other way out of this."

"Don't feel guilty about it," Chuck said as Jeremy untied his hands. "These two thugs had it coming to them. But now we'd better get things going, before Bersa finds out about this and tries to stop us."

"You're right Chuck. We don't have any time to waste."

Despite their urgency, Jeremy allowed himself to linger on one more moment and savor his first triumph. This had been his baptism of fire, and he had handled it well. Not only had he shown that he could handle himself when the bullets were flying, he also had shown that he could handle a gun with aplomb; and what was most satisfying, he had been able to exact justice for his colleague, McLoughlin. Thank you, God, for allowing me to accomplish this, he said to himself.

They collected their pistols and found their horses. There was not much they could do about the Crusaders' corpses, and they climbed into their saddles and set out for Jericho.

The time of reckoning had begun.

Chapter 4

They entered Jericho from the rear, picking their way down some dark lanes, until Chuck stopped and said, "Here we are, Reverend, Sheriff Dugan's office. This is the back door." They dismounted and left the horses standing free. "Let's go in," Chuck said. "I hope he's in his five senses."

"What do you mean?"

He lifted his hand as if he were holding a bottle and emptying its contents into to his mouth. "This."

"I get it. Do we really need him?"

"Yes we do, Reverend. There's no one else in Jericho who can bring all the folks together. There's no way we can do it ourselves. If we are seen in town, we stand out like sore thumbs."

"But can we trust Dugan?"

"We just have to. We've got no other choice."

They both pulled their guns, just in case, and Chuck turned the handle. Fortunately the door was unlocked, and they entered the dark building quietly, Chuck taking the lead since he was familiar with the place. They were in the jail portion, Jeremy noticed, as they were moving silently down a corridor with barred cells on both sides. No one was lodged there currently, which was no surprise, since order seemed to be maintained in Jericho simply by dispatching troublemakers with a bullet upon Bersa's command. The town was crime free, so to speak, if one ignored the main criminal and wrongdoer – Bersa himself.

The front office was illuminated by an oil lamp, and when they reached it, they found Sheriff Dugan slumped in his chair, indeed, with a more than half empty bottle propped up on the desk in front of him.

Chuck shook him by the shoulder. "Wake up, Sheriff."

Dugan, grey haired, with a deeply lined face and a belly, looked wasted and aged – more like a grandpa who should be taking care of his grandkids than an officer of the law who should be rooting out crime. When Chuck tried to wake him up, he just snorted, then kept on sleeping, and Chuck had to try again, whereupon he finally opened his eyes.

"What's going on?" he grunted. "Who are you? What do you want? And what's with the guns?" He pointed to the six shooters in their hands.

"Just a precaution," Chuck said. "I'm Chuck Harrison. You know me. And this is Reverend Cadoc."

"Cadoc?" Dugan suddenly became alert and sat up straight. "Bersa's been looking for him. He put the word out that he'll pay a bounty to anybody who'll bring him in."

"The Reverend has done nothing wrong," Chuck said. "He's simply an obstacle in Bersa's path, and that's no crime. He won't let him get away with all his lying, sinning and evil doings. In fact, that's why we're here today. Let the Reverend tell you in his own words."

Sheriff Dugan suddenly seemed to have sobered up. He took the bottle and stashed it away in a drawer of his desk. "All right, Reverend, I'll hear you out. But please," he added. "Put those guns away. They make me nervous."

"We will," Chuck said. "But no funny business, Sheriff."

"I promise."

They holstered their weapons, and Jeremy began to talk in a straight forward manner. "Here's what I propose, Sheriff. We get all the armed men in town together and arrest Bersa. We'll take over the Paradise and run the Crusaders out of town. If we all work together, it can be done."

"But we tried that before with McLoughlin, and didn't work. Bersa got the best of us, and now we're worse off than before."

"That's just the point," Chuck intervened. "We now have Reverend Cadoc, and he's got what it takes. McLoughlin had good intentions, I grant you, but he didn't have the mettle, being strictly the man of peace that he was. Friendly persuasion is not the way to deal with a man like Bersa. It takes toughness, and we have a tough man right here, Sheriff, to lead us."

"If this goes wrong, I'll be the first to be blamed by Bersa," Dugan said, still hesitant. Then he relented. "But I'm an old man and I don't have much to lose. And I love this town. Jericho's been good to me, and so I guess I owe this to the community." He addressed Jeremy, "Okay, what's my role in all of this?"

"Your role is to contact all the capable men in Jericho and ask them to come to a meeting."

"A meeting? Where?"

"Right here would be the best place. What do you think, Chuck?"

"I agree, Reverend."

"Is that okay with you Sheriff?"

"I guess so. When do you want the meeting?"

"As soon as possible. How about tomorrow night?"

"Tomorrow night is okay," the Sheriff said.

"Then that's how we do it. We'll meet an hour after sundown. But the meeting has to be kept secret. It can't reach Bersa's ears under any circumstances, is that understood?"

"Understood," the Sheriff affirmed. "I'll contact only those who I consider trustworthy."

"Okay, Sheriff."

They were about to leave, when someone rattled the door. "Dugan, are you awake? Or are you drunk as a skunk again?" The speaker chuckled and was joined by another man. "Put the bottle away and open up."

"Crusaders," Dugan commented in a low voice.

"That new Preacher is in town, Dugan," the first speaker barked from outside. "Someone saw him ride in. You need to help us find him."

"Just a minute. I'm coming." The Sheriff got up and ushered Jeremy and Chuck through a door into a dark room next to the office. "Wait here. I'll try to get rid of them," he said to Jeremy and Chuck, and then left to deal with the Crusaders outside.

Jeremy and Chuck found themselves in what seemed to be a parlor room equipped with a couch, an armchair, and a table – part of the Sheriff's living quarters apparently. As they were waiting tensely, listening to the muted sounds in the street, a door creaked open, and a female voice said, "Pa, where are you? What's going on outside? What's all the noise?"

It was a girl in her late teens, dressed in a nightgown, carrying a candle that cast a dim circle of light around her, enough to allow a glimpse of a comely figure, long blond locks and pretty features. Her eyes opened wide with surprise upon seeing them. "Who are you?"

"I'm Reverend Cadoc and this is Chuck Harrison. Who are you?"

"I'm Sally Dugan, the Sheriff's daughter. What are you doing here?"

"We met with your father."

"What for, may I ask?"

"To make plans."

"Plans for what?"

Jeremy hesitated. "I don't know whether I should discuss this with you. I'll let you father explain it."

"You can tell me," she insisted. "I'm my father's confidante. He shares all his affairs with me." She sounded very determined, exhibiting a maturity far beyond her age, which Jeremy found rather appealing. The only exposure he had had to the opposite sex in his young life was limited to women cut from a traditional cloth, women who were submissive to their men and took a passive role in human relations. An assertive female was a novel experience, which was refreshing. For the first time he felt an attraction to a member of the opposite sex that went beyond superficial friendship. There was a chemistry there, an electricity that was instant and exciting, and made him only too willing to tell her more. "Okay, here it is," Jeremy said. "The plan is to rid the town of Bersa. We need your father to help us execute it. He needs to get the townsfolk together for a meeting so we can organize everybody."

Sally, too, had felt excitement, and grabbing Jeremy's hand spontaneously, said enthusiastically, "That's great, Reverend! It's something that's been way overdue. I'm going to do everything I can to help." She looked at him warmly, and he felt a rush. He had never kissed a girl before, but he could have done so right there if Chuck hadn't intervened. "The Sheriff's coming in," he said. "Let's see what he tells us."

Earl Dugan looked somber and barely reacted to his daughter's presence. "They're looking all over for you," he said to Jeremy and Chuck. "It's a wonder they haven't come in here yet. You'd better leave before they do."

"Okay, Sheriff. We'll be back tomorrow night," Jeremy said.

"Yes, I'll get it all set up."

Jeremy turned to the Sheriff's daughter. "Good bye, Sally," he said with a warm glance, which she returned. "Good bye, Reverend." And both knew that a special bond had been established.

Not losing any more time, Jeremy and Chuck left the way they had arrived, down the corridor dividing the barred cells and out the rear. Their horses were still where they had left them standing, and they mounted quickly and made their way out of town through the back alleys, keeping a low profile.

At one point some shadowy riders yelled at them from the distance, but they paid no attention, and giving their horses the spurs, shot out into the night, leaving Jericho behind.

+   +   +

"We've turned over every stone, Reverend. There's no trace of him anywhere in town," Murdoch said, standing at the foot of Bersa's bed, with his hat in his hands. "What do you want us to do next?"

Bersa was annoyed. Cadoc -- that damn assistant! Several weeks had gone by and he thought that he had already left Jericho for good! But here he was still roaming about, making trouble. They had found the two dead guards at the cemetery; then, someone had spotted Cadoc in town, and it was easy to put two and two together. What was he up to next? "Any suggestions, Murdoch?"

Murdoch thought for a moment. Cadoc had been seen in the company of the Harrison boy, which could only mean one thing – that it was at the Harrisons where he had been hiding. But Murdoch didn't want to bring up his suspicions right here and now in the presence of Brandy, who was nestled against Bersa's chest. She was the boss' favorite, and he didn't want to risk his ire by bringing up the thorny subject. "I got an idea how to flush him out," he finally said.

"Yeah? How?"

"Just leave it to me. You can trust me."

Bersa knew that this was true. Murdoch had been with him the longest of any Crusader, and he had confidence in his smart thinking and absolute loyalty. Whatever he had up his sleeve, it had to be effective. Besides, Bersa had been about to enjoy himself with Brandy. Of his entire stable of fillies she was the best, and he didn't want to delay his pleasurable activities any longer.

"Okay, Murdoch, I'll leave it in your hands," he said. "And don't bother me again until you have some results." And waving Murdoch out of the room, he slapped Brandy on the buttock. "Let's have some fun, honey."

+   +   +

"I wonder how the Reverend and Chuck are doing, They've been gone for several hours now," Lena said, as she was darning a sock, sitting by the fireplace.

"Don't worry, Lena," her husband answered. "They're okay. They know what they're doing."

"Bersa is evil," Lena said. "Evil and dangerous."

"Yes, he is. He is a monster."

"And will we ever be able to see our baby again?"

"We will be, Lena, we will be. We have to keep up the faith."

"Oh Will," she exclaimed. "I don't know how long I'll be able to keep this up."

"You have to, Lena. You have to keep up the faith."

They were interrupted as the door burst open, and in marched Murdoch, Higgins, Polk and several other Crusaders.

"Where is he?" Murdoch demanded, as Lena gave a shriek. "Where's that preacher?"

"What preacher?" Will Harrison said meekly.

"You know who I'm talking about –Cadoc. They saw him in town with your boy, and that can only mean one thing – he's been hiding here."

"No…no… I don't know what you're talking about," Will stammered.

"He stole my horse and I found it here," one of the Crusaders said. "They claimed it was a stray. Now the truth comes out."

"Where is he?" Murdoch insisted, and neither Will nor Lena reacted, cowed as they were, and in a state of shock. "Well, if you don't want to tell me, you leave me no alternative."

Two gunshots rang out, and Will felt an impact in his chest and saw Lena buckle. "Lena," he called out as he slumped forward. Then a crackling sound reached his ears, accompanied by a loud snap as of a piece of wood, followed by several more snaps and a whole chain of small explosions. Smoke started swirling around them and red flames licked through the log structure of the cabin. "Lena, get down, " he cried out, with his last remaining energy grabbing her around the shoulders and pulling her to the floor as smoke built up solidly underneath the ceiling. "Crawl, Lena, crawl. Move your hands and legs. We've got to get out of here." And it was the last thing he managed to say before the burning roof and ceiling crashed down on them.

Chapter 5

There was an orange glow on the horizon. Jeremy knew that it could not be the rising sun: it did not come from the right direction – from too far to the north; besides there were still several hours left of the night even though they had made a time-consuming detour around the countryside in order to avoid the main road for fear of running into Bersa's men. There was only one possible explanation for the glow, suggested by the faint scent of charcoal pervading the atmosphere, an explanation he refused to acknowledge.

Chuck's intuition was identical. "There seems to be a fire up ahead, Reverend, don't you think?" And suddenly he became anxious. "God, it's not the farm, is it?"

"Let's pray it isn't.They did what they could to make the tired mounts that carried them go faster. As they advanced, the smell of burnt wood grew stronger, and the glow brighter. Ashes whirled past them, some entering their lungs and making them cough; finally, just as they turned around the last bend on the trail to the farm, they could hear the crackling – no longer noisily ecstatic, but sedately satisfied. Both farmhouse and barn were gutted, their roves caved in, although the fire was still eating away on the outer shell of each structure, finding the massive log walls an enduring source of nourishment.

"Good Lord, my folks," cried Chuck. He jumped off the horse and ran up to the burning remains of his home. But he was unable to enter; the flames were still high and the heat intense.

Jeremy came running up with a bucket from the well, full of water, which he threw on the fire. "Help me, Chuck. There's another bucket."

They went to work, trying to put out what remained of the fire, one of them filling the buckets, the other carrying them and emptying them, taking turns and continuing without interruption until at one point they stopped exhausted. They rested only a few moments, and pulling themselves together, went on with their labors. Eventually the flames died, and they were able to enter.

"Let me look, Chuck. You stay here," said Jeremy, wanting to spare his friend further pain.

But Chuck refused. "No, Reverend." He stepped into the smouldering embers of what only a few hours earlier had been his home. Going through the rubble with his bare hands, without thought of the burns he might suffer, raising a piece of charred wood here and clearing away the ashes there, Chuck searched frantically, trying to find some indication of what had happened, and in particular, of what had occurred to his parents.

Jeremy, who had entered behind Chuck, was asking himself the same thing. Where were Will and Lena? Perhaps Murdoch and his men -- the presumable perpetrators -- had taken them along as hostages so that they were safe and sound for the moment. Yes, that was it. He was already persuading himself of the certainty of this notion when, underneath the ashes, he saw something gleaming – apparently some insignificant metal object, perhaps a spoon, or a pair of scissors. Following an impulse to retrieve it, he bent down, but found that it was firmly embedded in the debris. He began to clear it away and suddenly realized what it was that he had found, yes, its identity became very clear, now that he was digging around the object, revealing its circular shape. Finally able to dislodge the ring, he polished it, and examining its inner rim, found his worst expectations confirmed by the engraving he found there: Lena 8-17-13. Hastily burrowing further, he uncovered some skeletal remains and shreds of clothing – evidently belonging to the old Harrison – and then a second skull and set of bones, and now he was completely sure that his previous theory concerning the whereabouts and condition of the old people had not been correct.

Without a word, he showed the wedding band to Chuck, who snatched it away from him to examine it. After doing so, Chuck looked at him questioningly, and then on the ground, and suddenly realizing the full significance of the discovered evidence, collapsed, sobbing.

Placing his arm around his shoulders, Jeremy tried to console him and to indicate that he accompanied him in his pain. "I'm going to say a prayer for them," said the Reverend, which he proceeded to do. Chuck seemed not to listen. Jeremy then went to look for some tools. Among the debris of the barn he found a pick and a spade, which were still serviceable, and began to excavate a hole. This job took quite a while. When he finished, Chuck had calmed down a bit, although he didn't feel up to helping with the burial of his parents' human remains. Jeremy had to do it by himself. Only when he had filled the grave with earth did he fetch Chuck so that he would be present during a brief sermon. Once that was done, Jeremy addressed Chuck, "Let's go, before Bersa's men come back."

But Chuck did not react. His eyes were still fixed on the grave, and he did not move.

"We have to go, Chuck" insisted Jeremy. "Let's go to the canyons."

Chuck remained motionless. "I'll get them," he suddenly blurted out, closing his fists. "I swear I'm gonna get them, and then I'll break their necks one by one." Abruptly he turned and started walking in the direction of Jericho.

Jeremy followed him and stopped him after a few steps. "Get a hold of yourself, Chuck. We can't take on the entire gang by ourselves.

Chuck looked at him in blind frustration. "Get out of my way."

"No, Chuck. First listen to me. I want to get these thugs as much as you. But it must be done the right way. Alone we won't succeed; but with the help of the people of Jericho I think we have a chance. We've got to be patient. We have to wait – at least until tomorrow when we have the meeting at the Sheriff's. And you – you've got to hang in there, as difficult as that may be."

Chuck did not seem convinced, but at last resigned himself. "May be you're right, Reverend. I'm not pleased that these animals run around free, without punishment, and me not being able to do anything about it, but after all, one day's wait is not much…"

"And it'll be worth the trouble, Chuck. We're going to get them soon, I promise, and then they'll pay for their awful sinning…"

They found their horses, which had been grazing nearby, and then they headed into the dawn of the breaking day and towards the mountains that loomed in the distance.

+   +   +

Sheriff Dugan opened his eyes, yawned, stretched and grunted; finally he raised himself up and got out of bed. It had been a strange night, he thought, as he put on his pants, shirt and boots: Cadoc, a minister of the Methodist Church, being hunted for killing several men and now wanting to organize what amounted to an armed rebellion. What a crazy preacher! The whole thing seemed fantastic in broad daylight – unsettling enough to warrant at least a small swig. With this in mind Earl Dugan went to the kitchen, where he kept his supply. He had just taken the bottle out of the cabinet and was about to put it to his lips, when Sally entered, looking fresh and bright in a colorful dress.

"Pa! You promised to stop drinking. You know that it's bad for you."

"Just one taste, little girl. Just a little something to get me going."

"You don't need anything to get you going, nor anything the rest of the day, especially now that you've got new obligations. Reverend Cadoc needs your help."

"Cadoc? What's he to me! That young preacher is plumb crazy. To rise up against Bersa and his gunslingers? Impossible. It's never going to work."

"You don't understand, Pa. Bersa's powerful, that's true, but he's able to bully this town around only because of folks who think like you. Somebody like Cadoc can help us get over our fears and beat Bersa. I've got great faith in the new Reverend, and I want you to have faith in him too."

Earl Dugan was amazed at her fervor and suddenly remembered the hand-pressing between her and Jeremy the night before, an act which had not escaped his notice. Was his little girl more than just civic-minded in extolling Cadoc's virtues? Whatever were her motives, he didn't agree with her reasoning – didn't want to agree with it, now that he had had more time to think it over. "Listen to me, baby, why should I get involved in all this? We don't have it bad here, the two of us. Bersa treats us fair as long as I do what he wants. I'm making a living. It's not my fight, really."

"Then why did you humor the Reverend last night? Why did you agree to the meeting?"

"They came in with their guns drawn, and it's hard to argue with that."

"Was it just their guns? Or was it because you felt ashamed?"

"Ashamed about what?"

"Ashamed about the way you handle your job. You put up with Bersa, but you don't like him any more than the rest of us. Well, now you've got a chance to do something about it and win back your pride."

"My pride?"

"Yes, Pa, your pride. There's not much left of it."

Earl Dugan was shocked. Never before had he seen his daughter talk so forcefully.

Presently she apologized. "I'm sorry, Pa. I didn't mean it. I don't know what came over me. I didn't mean to hurt you." She came to where he stood and leaned her head against his shoulder.

"It's all right, baby. Don't worry. I've forgotten about it already."

But he knew that his daughter was right. He had failed to face his responsibilities for too long now, and perhaps the time had come at last to make up for his negligence. He certainly owed as much to the people of Jericho. Thoughtfully he replaced the cork on the bottle he was holding in his hand and stashed it away in the cabinet. "You know, I think you're right, Sally. With a leader like Cadoc we might have a chance to succeed. Now bring me something to eat."

While he was having breakfast at the table, he continued their conversation. "Now let's see...... Who am I going to round up for the meeting? There's Derryl Adams, on account of him having been mayor at one time; I guess I'll find him at his store. Maynard Stovall, at the bank ...he was a member of the town council before Bersa dissolved it. There's Doc Browser; he, too, was a councilman at one time. Bill Clark, at the livery stable, ought to have a say, and I suppose I ought to invite Pete Thompson."

"Pete Thompson, the blacksmith?"

"He's the only one with any spunk left. He can help us a lot."

"What about Abe Hutchison?"

"The undertaker? I'll include him too. He's got a steady mind."

"And Johnny Shine?"

"That blabbermouth? What use is he going to be?"

"He's a clown," Sally conceded. "But there's a lot of folks going in and out of his place, getting haircuts and shaves, including the Crusaders. He knows everything that goes on in town, and that might come in handy."

"All right, little girl. I'll include him too, then."

He ate the rest of his breakfast, thinking about how he would approach them. It would not be easy. Cadoc had said that he wanted capable men, but in reality there weren't any around. These men were all cowards, with the exception of Thompson, the blacksmith, and he couldn't blame them; they were only ordinary human beings, terrorized by forces beyond their control. It would be necessary to make panthers out of these pussycats in order to overcome the oppressors. But he would leave that mostly up to Cadoc. His own task, formidable in itself, would simply be to bring them together with the preacher and expose them to his persuasive efforts.

"Sally, honey, I'm leaving," he called out to his daughter, who had momentarily gone to some other part of the house. Taking advantage of her absence, he went to the cabinet and sneaked a swig after all – to top off the breakfast – and thus fortified, went to the front door. "I won't be back till late," he said to Sally, who now arrived. "You mind the house and take messages. And come to get me if there is anything important."

"Yes, Pa."

He kissed her on the forehead and left in order to carry out his mission.

+   +   +

Wiping the sweat off her brow, Sally Dugan took a step backward, out of the intense heat emitted by the cast-iron stove on which she was preparing dinner. "Lord, what drudgery," she said and pushed back some strands of yellow hair. It was at times like this that she wished she still had a mother, who could take care of the household chores and give her an opportunity to grow up more normally; but immediately she felt guilty about her unloving notion. It had been ten years now – Sally watched the bubbling pots and was transported back to the past in her memory – ten years that her mother had died. What of, nobody had ever sufficiently explained to her at the time, but she realized now that it had been as a consequence of a miscarriage. She remembered that night, the bearded doctor entering the bedroom, the screams from inside, the blood-soaked towels and bandages that were brought out, and her father's mournful cries. At last he had come out of the room, guided by the doctor, crestfallen and seemingly a changed man.

Soon after the burial they had moved: haunted by the tragedy, her father had taken to drink and had become ineffective in his job as a federal Marshall – she remembered the problems he had with the judges and other officials. They went west and lived in a number of places, staying in a succession of hotel rooms, her father making a living at various odd jobs, wanting to forget, until they reached

Jericho, where he landed his present job – the perfect stooge for Bersa, she knew now. There was no law-work to be done in Jericho: the citizenry was kept in check by Bersa and his men. All her father had to do was to remain indifferent, registering and listening to their complaints on the one hand, and on the other hand be a discreet transmitter of Bersa's wishes. They had lived like this since their arrival; she had run the household, carrying out what had formerly been her mother's functions, while her father served as Bersa's patsy, his spirit gone, his body increasingly corrupted by drink.

But now there was new hope. She thought of Jeremy, his rugged, handsome looks, his proud spirit, which could not be subdued by the tyrannical Bersa – a fiery stallion which would not submit to the rein or the whip, and would not allow himself to be imprisoned, but which would jump all hurdles, stomp down all obstacles, and bring things back to their natural rhythm. Sally felt exalted. It was indeed a great blessing that the Reverend Cadoc had come. He would re-establish justice in town. He would bring peace and dignity back to the people. And….she hardly dared to acknowledge the thought… would he also take further notice of her? She remembered his warm glance the night before, and her hand grasping his in silent communication, and the thought made her feel happy. She suddenly realized that she was longing to see him again, longing to look into his soulful dark eyes once more, to stand close to him and be enveloped by that warmth and strength that emanated from his body and being, and she let herself be entranced by the sweetness of the idea for a long while. When her father entered from the street, she was brought back to the realities of the steaming kitchen.

"Howdy, girl. Anything good on the stove?" He threw his hat on the table and came to look at the pots as usual, but he did not seem to be really interested. His face was funereal.

"What's the matter, Pa? Problems with the meeting?"

Her father shook his head. "No, Sally, it's not that. Adams, Stovall, the Doc, Clark and the others – I got them all to come, though it wasn't easy. I beat around the bush some – didn't tell them the real reason for our little get-to-gether; that's up to Cadoc. I just let them know that it was a matter of extreme importance for their businesses. They'll show up for sure."

"Then what's troubling you, Pa? What happened?"

Instead of answering, her father went straight to the storage cabinet to retrieve the bottle.

"Don't do any drinking, Pa, please. Whatever it is that's bothering you, tell me about it."

This time he did not heed her; he took a long draught and then another, and only after having thus indulged himself, he spoke, wiping his mouth. "You know the Harrison place, about five miles out of town?"

"Sure do. Nice family. It's a shame what happened to their daughter, Brandy."

"Yes, it's a shame – a crying shame – but what happened to the old folks and their homestead is even worse."

"What are you saying, Pa?"

"The farm burned to the ground last night."

"No! I can't believe it." Sally sat down, upset. "How could such a thing happen?"

"Murdoch and his cutthroats." Earl Dugan set the bottle down after another drink. "They set fire to it on Bersa's orders."

"How horrible! But why, Pa? Why would Bersa want a thing like that? He's already taken the Harrisons' daughter. They pay their dues like anyone else in town. Why would he punish them even more?"

"There's something you and I didn't know, girl. Cadoc's been staying with the Harrisons for the last few weeks, hiding out. Bersa didn't know about it either until last night when Cadoc was seen in Chuck's company."

"What about old Will and Lena?"

Her father hesitated. At last he said, "They died in the fire. Bersa wanted to make an example of them."

"Oh, good Lord!" Sally began to sob. Finally, through a veil of tears, she asked, "And Chuck and the Reverend , did they also die in the flames?"

Her father looked at her reassuringly. "I don't think so, though I can't be completely certain. When I went out to the site this afternoon, I didn't see a trace of them, dead or alive. But I did find two graves with two crosses that had the names of Will and Lena cut into them, and I don't think that was Murdoch's work."

Sally looked at him expectantly, drying her tears. "Whose was it?"

"Wouldn't surprise me if it was Chuck and Cadoc who buried them, which would mean they're alive. But I don't have any idea at all where they are. Could be anywhere – may be with one of Chuck's friends in town, or out in the country. Who knows?"

Sally's mood brightened a bit, in spite of her pain over the Harrisons. "Oh, I don't care where they are at this moment, as long as they're safe. Without the Reverend, what would we do? I thank God that he has protected him."

"Now, hold your horses," her father cautioned. "What I told you is only guesswork, remember that. They may not have gotten away after all, and may have fallen victims to the flames, or to Bersa in some other way. Bersa never gives up. So don't be so sure, girl; I don't want to build up your hopes for nothing." He sounded tender. "Wait until tomorrow. Tomorrow at the meeting we'll find out for sure."

"Will Cadoc be there, Pa?" she could not refrain from asking.

Her father took another swig and shrugged. "Let's hope so." And he sat down at the table to have the dinner that she had prepared for him.

Chapter 6

Sitting motionless in the saddle, Murdoch scanned the horizon. Through his fieldglasses he could see every crack and depression in the mesas which were jutting out into the open range like the bulwarks of a giant fortress into the sea; he could make out every rock and sage bush in the passageways that led into the canyons. No movement anywhere, except the fleeting shadow of a hawk which passed through his field of vision briefly. He handed his glasses to Higgins, who was next to him. "Here, you take a look."

Higgins did as asked, taking his time.

"Well, what do you think?"

"They could be in any one of them canyons," Higgins said, handing back the glasses. "It ain't gonna be easy to track them down."

Murdoch nodded. "We've got ten men," he said. "Enough to make a thorough check. You take four, and I'll take the rest. This time the preacher won't escape. Go on and pick the ones you want."

"Mahoney, Southworth, Curtin, Polk," Higgins called out, and the named guards detached themselves from the group that had been waiting in back. "You fellows come with me."

But one of the men balked. "We're going with you?" he asked belligerently. "I ain't got no taste for it. You ain't fit to be a leader of men." It was Curtin, slight of build, with the stubborn face of a rodent. He backed his horse away.

Higgins turned pale. "Why, you bastard...." His hand went to the holster, but the other was already pointing his gun at him.

Murdoch interceded. "What's the matter, Curtin? Did Higgins step on your toes? There's no use insulting or killing each other. That preacher is doing enough of that already. We need every man right now. Let's settle this thing reasonably."

The two men kept staring at each other, Curtin grimly, Higgins treacherously calm.

"Come on now, Curtin," Murdoch urged. "What is it?"

"He knows," Curtin spewed. "I don't have to spell it out for him....The spooky way he treats the dames... it's no secret to anyone. Not even the salon whores want any dealings with him any longer. So what does he do now? He preys on what belongs to others....."

"What are you talking about?"

"This son of a bitch tried to have his way with my girl last night. I caught him at it and slugged him. He said he would get me on the bad side of you, Murdoch, if I let on about it. But I don't care any more."

"What have you got to say about that?" Murdoch asked Higgins.

Higgins was calm, stroking his stubbly chin with one hand, resting the other on the saddle horn in front of his bulging abdomen. "I say that....," he began, but before finishing the phrase, his right hand slipped into an inside pocket of his jacket and retrieved a Derringer, which he fired at Curtin. The latter also fired, but his bullet whirled through empty space, for Higgins, with surprising agility, had dived off his horse and was rolling over on the ground. A second round from the Derringer finished off Curtin, who slumped in the saddle as his horse reared up, tossing him to the ground.

"…I say that he's a liar," Higgins finished his sentence, getting up and dusting himself off. "The truth is that he himself is the troublemaker. Look at him." He turned over Curtin's face with his boot tip. "Ain't he the ugliest thing you ever laid eyes on? There ain't a female in the whole territory that would put up with him willingly. The fact is that it was he who went after one of my own chosen lovelies, and I because I'm kind and generous, didn't make him bite the dust sooner. But," he continued, "let's not waste time with this kind of nonsense. Let's get going before that preacher slips away again." He mounted and waved to the remaining three men designated to go with him.

The three did not react immediately but looked to Murdoch, who sat on his horse hesitant, trying to deal with the situation. He knew that Curtin probably had been in the right: Higgins was known to have a sadistic streak, and if he had attempted to rape Curtin's paramour, it wouldn't have been the first time that he had committed such an act. But it was Higgins whom he, Murdoch, needed now – his aggressiveness and cunning – and it wasn't important that the brute had murdered the other man without justification. Unable to afford any further delay, Murdoch motioned to the three guards to join the fat man. "We'll talk about this later," he said to

Higgins. "You and your men go ahead. If you come across anything, fire three shots."

"Sure thing, Murdoch. It shouldn't take us long to catch up with them, if they're here." Higgins smirked, and slapping his horse, galloped off, leading his little platoon towards the first mesa.

Murdoch had the remaining guards load Curtin's corpse onto the riderless horse, and ordered one of them to conduct the gruesome cargo back to town. Then he turned his mount towards the second mesa. "Let's go, boys," he said. "Let's get that preacher."

+   +   +

They had been unmistakably gunshots – two high-pitched pops interrupted by one low, more full-bodied blast, followed by total silence.

"A Derringer and a Colt," Chuck commented laconically. "The Derringer won out."

They were squatting at the edge of the platform that protruded in front of the cave in which they had spent the night. There was a patch of grass there, and their mounts, tied to the branches of a bush near the cave entrance, were feeding upon it in tranquility. Their hideout was suspended above the canyon at an altitude of some 200 feet, invisible to anyone who might approach below.

"Was it Murdoch and his gang?" Jeremy questioned.

"Could be," said Chuck. "But who fired the Derringer?"

"Who knows. We've got to be cautious from now on." Jeremy got up, and with his boot destroyed the glowing embers by which they had been sitting. "I wonder how long it will take them to come around here. I hope we can hold out at least until tonight."

"I think so, Reverend," commented Chuck. "Not even a native scout could track us to this spot. But I'd sure feel more comfortable if we were better armed."

Jeremy touched the Colt in his holster. "You don't have any faith in our guns?"

"I do, but is it enough against a small army? Of course, if everything fails, I've got this," Chuck said, producing his knife, "but it isn't gonna do much good against a barrage of gunfire." He flung it at a piñon that grew twisted from a niche. The weapon remained quivering in its slim trunk.

Jeremy retrieved it and playfully tested the razor-sharp blade with his thumb. With considerable respect, he returned the lethal instrument to its owner. "You can do damage with this," he said and went on, "The only thing we can do for now is wait and keep a watch. Let's see what the afternoon will bring."

Their patience was tested for more than an hour when the sound of clattering hooves down in the canyon startled them. At once they threw themselves flat on the ground, taking cover behind some big rocks. The noise grew louder, and before long four riders came around the nearest bend, following the course of the river bed – dry at this time of the year, except for a small trickle of water which carved its way down thc middle in a crooked line.

"Looks like Higgins, Polk and two others I don't know," Jeremy said in a low voice, although he and Chuck were too far removed from the canyon floor to be overheard. "Let's see what they're up to."

The four riders came to a halt at a point where the canyon expanded to form an arena. They spread out to check everything, pursuing the natural paths that led some distance up the canyon sides, examining some rocky overhang here, a niche or crevice – of which there were many – there. One of the Crusaders – Jeremy realized it was Polk – had chosen to concentrate on the area immediately below the cave. Steadily he was ascending among the boulders, leading his mount by the reins, his eyes fixed on the ground before him. The path ended in a confusion of rocks and rubble, and Polk stopped to scan the canyon side farther up, as Jeremy and Chuck watched with apprehension. Apparently he did not notice anything suspicious and turned to head back down, but then he stopped and bent down to examine something on the ground. Again he gazed up the slope and resumed his climb, now leaving his horse behind and following a zig-zag path slowly but steadily.

"What were you saying about a native scout not being able to find us?" Jeremy whispered to Chuck.

"Polk's smarter than I thought," Chuck whispered back.

"Nonetheless I'll outdo him. See that rifle?" Jeremy pointed to the weapon sticking out of the saddle holster on the side of Polk's horse.

"I do, Reverend."

"I'm going to grab it."

"Are you crazy, Reverend? It's too risky…"

"It doesn't seem too difficult, Chuck. I can go and return in no time, hiding behind the rocks. Polk is not even going to realize what happened."

"What if he comes all the way up here?"

"In that case you've got your knife, and as a last resort your gun. Besides, by that time I'll have the rifle and can help you."

"Okay, Reverend. I reckon it's worth the trouble. But be quick."

Chuck watched him disappear among the boulders, slip down the canyon side to the left of Polk and approach the latter's horse from behind, while Polk himself was coming up more slowly from the right, pausing once in a while, but closing in gradually. Chuck gripped his knife tightly. He glanced across to the horses by the cave entrance and ordered them to be quiet, then directed his attention downhill once more. He could see Jeremy slip out behind Polk's mount now and inch his way up to the animal, which stirred a little but seemed otherwise cooperative. There was a moment of tension as the Reverend laid his hand on the rifle. The mount reared up slightly; then Cadoc took possession of the weapon and vanished among the rocks.

Polk was very close now, so close that Chuck could see the puzzled look on his face. However, the man still had not detected the ledge nor the cave behind it. He was apparently following his intuition rather than any firm clues. He stopped to catch his breath and, perhaps, to decide whether to go on.

It was then that one of the horses by the cave gave a snort – ever so gently but loud enough to alert Polk. The latter cocked his head to listen more intently, then shook it. "Sounds like a critter," he mumbled and started towards the ledge. Chuck poised himself on his toes like a cat, ready for the attacking leap, prepared to plunge the knife into the other's chest, when the silence was broken by a prolonged neighing that filled the canyon from one end to the other, followed by the clatter of hooves and the noise of falling rocks and debris. It was Polk's horse, which was taking off down the slope at break-neck speed, apparently spooked by something unseen. Polk reacted at once, turning and scampering down the hill, his companions appearing one by one and stepping in the path of the stampeding mount. Chuck turned around to his own horse and that of Jeremy near the cave to keep those animals calm.

Down the slope, Jeremy lay behind a boulder, watching Polk stumble past him at close range. Just in time, he thought. A moment later and he would have discovered Chuck. Jeremy was still holding the rifle, which he had used as a club in order to hit Polk's horse, but now he turned it around in its proper position and cradled it between shoulder and cheek, training it on the black-clad guards below. He and Chuck were still far from safe. Polk's cronies had managed to arrest the runaway horse, and Jeremy could hear their muffled voices as they conferred with Polk, who had reached them. Polk checked his empty saddle holster, evidently aware of the missing rifle; then he pointed up the slope, and they all glanced upward.

Here they come again, Jeremy thought and accommodated himself more comfortably in the brambles behind the boulder, cocking the hammer, waiting for them to start towards him. But fortunately things did not come to that point. Suddenly, from the distance, three evenly-spaced reports could be heard, fired by a single gun – a signal which had an electrifying effect on the four Crusaders. They whirled around in the direction from which the shots had issued and from which further intermittent gunfire rang across now. Then Higgins motioned, and they all mounted their horses and departed at a full gallop, soon disappearing around the nearest bend of the canyon.

Unsure as to the reasons for this unexpected turn of events, Jeremy, keeping himself covered, climbed up to the cave, where he was received by a vastly relieved Chuck.

"Reverend, you saved us," Chuck exclaimed. "I was just about to give Polk his last…..What 'd you do to that old nag? You scared the daylights out of it."

"Just nudged it a little. But that wasn't what drove off the Crusaders. It was the gunfire. Can you hear it? They're still keeping it up….maybe a couple of miles away. I wonder what's going on."

"It's probably Murdoch and the rest of the gang," Chuck guessed. "They must have run into some sort of trouble."

Jeremy nodded. "Whatever it is, we'd better keep a low profile until tonight. I just hope they won't think of coming back here."

"There's no telling, Reverend. Polk had his suspicions, and he might come back for his missing rifle. But may be he'll forget about it, with everything that's happening over there." He motioned towards the faintly audible gunbattle that was continuing in the distance. "My feeling is we should stay right here." He pointed at the weapon in Jeremy's hand. "At least we have this now. Makes me feel a whole lot better."

Jeremy looked at his booty and for the first time inspected it closely. It was a .44-40 Winchester with a 24-inch barrel capable of firing fifteen rounds – an almost brand-new rifle: Bersa kept his men excellently outfitted. To hold the weapon in his hand, to contemplate its gleaming barrel, its delicately tooled firing mechanism – so brilliantly designed – and to sense the barely harnessed power it contained gave Jeremy a rare aesthetic thrill which he had never experienced before. Suddenly he too felt powerful, in command of the situation, indestructible and ready for anything, absolutely certain that he would defeat the mighty Bersa – and he savoured the sensation.

"Yes, we do have this rifle," he echoed Chuck's words. "Isn't it a beauty?" He went to the cave entrance, picked out a blanket and rolled the gun into it very carefully. Having completed this task, he returned to the ledge that overlooked the canyon and settled down next to Chuck, placing the bundle on the ground next to himself. "Let's wait," he said. "It won't be much longer now."

And together they continued their vigil.

+   +   +

They were Apaches, and there were may be six or seven of them – a hunting party most likely, though there wasn't much to be hunted in these parts except a few lizards, and with some luck, perhaps a rabbit or two. They had barricaded themselves in around the water hole, and Murdoch knew that it would be difficult to flush them out just between himself and his three men, even though they seemed to be carrying only old-fashioned muzzle loaders and bows and arrows. But Higgins and his men ought to be responding to his signal soon, and with their forces combined, they should find a way to deal with the problem on hand. Meanwhile they would keep those pitiful redskins in line with an occasional round of their own.

"Hey, Ferris," he hissed to the man who was kneeling behind a bush to his right. "Keep up the fireworks. Pass the word to the others. Higgins and his boys ought to be around in no time."

This message was promptly relayed and resulted in a sudden surge in the cacophony that filled the atmosphere – the sharp cracking of the handguns, the whining of ricocheting bullets, counterpointed by the deep, cannon-like roars of the muzzle-loaders -- all of which had no apparent visible effect. But Murdoch noticed a flutter behind the trees around the water hole: one of the braves apparently had been hit, an encouraging development. Presently he was further heartened by the arrival of Higgins, who, followed by Polk and the other two men, came scuttling up on his belly through the grass and rocks.

Catching his breath, the fat man took cover next to Murdoch. "You found Cadoc?"

"No, these are Apaches. Looks like they strayed off their reservation. They're dug in pretty tight back there. It'll be a fair job to get them out."

"Send some men around the back, and we'll have them in a lock," Higgins suggested.

"I don't think that'll work. Look at those canyon walls. They're too steep for anyone to pass."

Higgins knew that Murdoch was right. The canyon walls rose almost vertically to a height of perhaps 300 feet. "Then why don't we simply take them head-on. Them redskins ought to be easy pickings."

"I don't want to take any chances," Murdoch said. "I don't want any of our boys to get hurt if I can help it. It isn't worth it."

Higgins nodded. "There's a way of getting around the risk, though….."

"What are you saying? What way?"

" By arranging a truce."

"A what?"

"You heard right -- a truce. Them reservation Indians are peaceful nowadays. They don't like to fight. So why not make friends with them?"

"We can't do that, Hig'. What's gotten into you? You know that Bersa wants to get rid of as many as possible, and the fact that they're of their territory gives us the perfect excuse. Besides, this way we won't go back to town empty-handed since we still haven't found the smallest trace of Cadoc yet."

"Take it easy, now," Higgins appeased Murdoch. "You got me altogether wrong. What I had in mind wasn't friendship till-death-do-us-part. It was more like a temporary deal, a short ceasefire. That way we'll be able to get face-to-face with them, and once we've gotten to that point, who's to say what can happen? No peace lasts forever, if you get my drift." He gave Murdoch a look pregnant with meaning.

Murdoch caught on. "You're a sly old fox, Hig'," he said with a grin. "What you're suggesting sounds workable. Bring me Buckeye; he knows how to deal with them 'skins. Get him over here and we'll figure out a plan of action."

+   +   +

Near the water hole, Falling Moon leaned back behind the sparse trunk of a mesquite tree, which he was using for cover, and opened up his ammunition bag – formerly his medicine pouch – made of deerskin, intricately stitched, which had been passed down to him from his father and father's father, to stuff his tired musket with yet another charge. What for he was not sure, for the intermittent, badly aimed rounds he dispatched with it, seconded by the other two guns and the arrows of the others in his band, could hardly do more than give their attackers to understand that they were still alive, and not willing to give up completely. It would be only a matter of time before they were overrun. Why he and his men had been assaulted in the first place was a mystery to him. His tribe had given up warfare long ago, after they had been defeated by the bluecoats. They had been displaced from their rich hunting grounds and had been brought here to languish in the red desert. They had tried to survive by growing some meager crops on the barren land, and never fired another shot at the white man. How could they have? There was no spirit left in the braves. If they did use their simple weapons at all, it was only to supplement their starvation-level food supplies with an occasional bite of meat, as had been the purpose of the present outing. The white agents that came by the reservation now and then to check on them, knew this, and so did the settlers in the nearby town. All the more amazing that he and his braves should have been attacked so ferociously by the men in black, who had come upon them so suddenly. Red Eagle, his cousin, had been shot in the neck at the outset –he had seen his head jerk and dangle sideways before he collapsed – and was lying out in the open, only a few feet away. Not a proud warrior's death by any means! Rather this was the work of merciless butchers who were killing some wretched animals. But why?

Unable to fathom the reasons and purpose of this tragedy, Falling Moon raised the gun, which he had finished loading, and aimed it above the corpse and at the line of concealed enemies beyond. He was ready to pull the trigger and let go yet another charge but detained himself when from the opposite camp, out of the bushes and rocks, emerged a fluttering white rag. A peace signal? Finally! Finally the white men had come to their senses.

Falling Moon motioned to his companions to hold their fire. A moment later a man emerged from the opposite camp, waving a truce flag tied to a branch; he sauntered out into the open cautiously and came to a halt midway between the two firing lines. Having planted the pole into the ground before him, the man began to shout something, and Falling Moon recognized his own language, though spoken with an uncommon accent.

"You can come out, brothers," the man intoned. "Let us bury our weapons. We do not want bloodshed. It was all an error on our part,"

Falling Moon was glad to hear these conciliatory words, but he remained wary. "An error? How can that be?"

"We were looking for someone else – two white fugitives who have broken our laws. We thought that they were with you."

"There are no white men in our band. We are Apaches from the reservation. We are simple hunters."

"We are aware of that now," the man by the makeshift flagpole said. "You don't have white men's weapons. Let's make peace between your party and ours."

Falling Moon felt extremely relieved, though his instincts would not let him cast caution to the wind altogether. Could his adversaries and their spokesman indeed be trusted? He had to take a chance on it; it was the only way to save his band from certain defeat. His mind made up, he stepped out from behind the mesquite tree and slowly approached the negotiator, carrying his musket with him. As he reached the man, he saw that he was a dark-complexioned individual, whose fine black hat and well-fitting black suit could not cover up the fact that he was one of their own race, or at least shared their blood; his copper skin, dark pupils and wide cheekbones gave him away. He looked emaciated, with hollow cheeks and a deeply creased forehead, complemented by unshaven stubbles. The man stretched out his hand, and Falling Moon hesitantly shook it, in the white man's fashion.

"Again I apologize; we never had any intention of attacking your band," said the Crusader. "But let me ask you, have you seen two white men around? One tall, and the other short, both of them dark-haired?" As he spoke, the man emitted a pungent aroma which Falling Moon knew to be alcohol.

"No, we have been here since morning and haven't seen anybody."

"Well, then, we have to look elsewhere. Please accept my apologies. I beg your forgiveness also on behalf of my friends here." He was referring to the other guards, who, led by Murdoch and Higgins, had approached innoculously, guns stashed in their holsters.

Falling Moon knew that they were waiting for some form of acceptance of their apology, but he did not grant it. He sensed that his own men were drawing up behind him too now.

"Well, can we consider the matter settled now? Can we part as friends?" the negotiator asked, sounding a bit impatient.

Falling Moon hesitated. "You killed one of our braves," he said somberly, pointing to the corpse in back. "How will you repair the damage?"

There was a moment of awkward silence. The negotiator conferred with his companions, and after a brief discussion, faced Falling Moon once more. "We're extremely sorry about the unfortunate mishap," he said. "And we will of course give a compensation to the brave's family. Come into Jericho with us, all of you, and we shall work out the details."

"There is no possible compensation for a human life," Falling Moon said reproachfully. "But we are a beaten people and shall have to accept your terms. However, I warn you, we shall also direct a strong protest to your government in Washington, and do whatever we can to bring justice to bear concerning this terrible crime." He motioned to his braves. "We shall see you in Jericho," he said, and without another word, started back towards the water hole at the head of his little band.

But the negotiator tried to detain them. "Let's go into town together, brothers," he said. "We shall be honored to escort you."

Falling Moon turned around and looked at him contemptuously. "We are neither women, children nor …," he hesitated, "nor prisoners. We may live on a reservation, but within that system we're free – as free as you are in your world. We don't need anyone's help." Surrounded by his braves, he proceeded towards the water hole and towards their horses, and had no intention of stopping again. There was no reason to believe that the whites would detain them any further.

The explosions of the guns behind them were so closely coordinated that they seemed almost one single blast issued from some monstrous weapon. Falling Moon felt a searing pain in the center of his back and a moment later found himself face-down on the ground, vaguely aware of the writhing bodies of his braves around him, caught up in the convulsions of a dance of death. Summoning all his remaining energies, he made an extreme effort to turn over and face his aggressors, and indeed he managed to prop himself up into a sitting position with the aid of his old gun, to which he had been clinging all the while. He even managed to cock the hammer and fire a shot, but it had no other effect than to blow the swarthy negotiator's Stetson off, liberating a straggly mess of hair. There was another volley of shots from the row of executioners, and it put a sudden end to the grizzly ballet around him. Falling Moon sensed a pain in his chest, and then found himself coughing up blood. The last thing he laid his eyes on was the negotiator's face, distorted by a diabolical grin, framed by the black aura of his billowing locks – a messenger of death, who stood facing him with his smoking pistol in his hand.

Betrayed by one of our own, he thought. It seemed a fitting end indeed to his miserable existence.

Chapter 7

The distant guns had been silent for some time, and the dusk that had been engulfing the two men increasingly, was turning into night.

"Time to go, Chuck. Looks like everything is clear down below."

"Right, Reverend. We shouldn't arrive late at the meeting. There doesn't seem to be anybody left to stop us."

They stretched their extremities, then saddled the horses and picked up their sparse gear. Leading their mounts by the reins, they cautiously descended into the black depths of the canyon. Arriving at the bottom, they found that eyesight was no longer of any avail; they had to navigate by sound alone, and perhaps even more than that, by intuition.

"You take the lead," Jeremy said to Chuck, who he could sense by his side. "You know the way better than I do."

"Don't worry, Reverend. I can find my way out of here blind-folded. But stay close behind me."

They mounted, and Jeremy let him go ahead; then he spurred his own horse, intent on not losing Chuck, but at the same time keeping a certain distance so as to avoid colliding with the animal in front. They continued in this way for a while, advancing at a walking pace, over bedrock and rubble, once or twice fording the river which was hardly more than a creek, pausing now and then to listen for anyone who might be approaching from the opposite direction. But there was nothing more to be heard than the quiet trickling of the running water and the occasional hooting of an owl or howling of a coyote. Then visibility suddenly improved – Jeremy was able to distinguish Chuck's outline before him, set off against the vague silhouette of a broadening countryside beyond. He seemed to be able to distinguish trees and bushes, the uneven shapes of hillocks, and a diffused horizon which merged with a piece of the sky marked by the dim needle points of the stars. At last the entire panorama opened up, and the sky turned into a vast dome studded with a myriad of sparkling dots. They had reached the canyon exit.

Chuck stopped his mount, waiting until Jeremy arrived.

"Well, we're out of the trap, Reverend. If we run into any of Bersa's men now, we'll be able to dodge them easily." He pointed to the horizon. "Over there is Jericho. We'll ride along the foot of the mesas for a spell and then cut across the range towards town. That's the fastest way."

"You're the expert, Chuck. Let's not waste any time."

On they went, along the indicated route, skirting the first mesa, which loomed massively above them, until before long they reached the mouth of another canyon that needed to be crossed.

"I've got my bearings now, Chuck," Jeremy said, recognizing familiar landforms. "Let's speed it up. We don't want to keep those town elders waiting."

"If you say so, Reverend."

Giving his horse the spurs, Jeremy shot ahead of Chuck, crossing the canyon mouth at a gallop. It was a real joy to give free rein to the animal after the lengthy walk – a physical release, accompanied by a liberation of the tensions that had built up in him during the long hours in their hideout. At last they were on their way, bolting through the night without restraints, launched towards action and towards the accomplishment of their goals! Jeremy could hear Chuck's horse behind him. He thought now that near the horizon, perhaps three or four miles away, he could distinguish the outskirts of Jericho, and letting out an excited yell, dug the spurs into his horse's flanks even harder. But his euphoria was short-lived.

He did not notice the bulk on the ground until he was practically on top of it. It was suddenly there and under him without warning, as if projected there instantaneously by some weird magic. Jeremy pulled back the reins violently, causing his horse to rear up with a scream, and had he not grabbed the saddle horn, he would surely have been thrown off. It was too late to move over, out of Chuck's path – the collision was inevitable. Jeremy felt the hard impact of Chuck's steed, heard the pained neighing and Chuck's alarmed shouts, felt his own mount swaying and tilting, almost keeling over, then going to its knees and scrambling, and finally pulling away from the spot, running for a short distance, striving to regain its balance, until it stood firmly on its legs again. At once Jeremy jumped off the trembling animal and went back to the scene of the near-accident, where he found Chuck, who was also dismounting.

"Did you get hurt, Chuck?"

"I'm fine, Reverend. But, what's going on? What made you break so suddenly?"

"I couldn't help it, Chuck. Look," he pointed to the mysterious bulk on the ground. "That's what spooked my horse."

"What is it?"

Jeremy shrugged. "Let's see." With some apprehension he approached the dark form. It couldn't be a shrub or a log – his horse would have simply jumped over it. The object seemed strange and disturbing: it had been completely motionless; but still there had been some movement – the suggestion of a flickering flame, ghost-like, more abstract than real – and it was that which might have contributed to his horses excessive reaction. Now that Jeremy approached it, again it seemed nothing more than a simple bulk, and when he bent down to examine it, he discovered that it was in fact a human being, a man dressed in deerskin rags, with braided hair and sharply-cut, bony features – an Indian, who was apparently dead.

"He's an Apache, from the reservation," commented Chuck, who came up behind. "His name's Falling Moon. I've seen him around here when he was hunting. But he seems finished."

But Jeremy, checking the man's pulse, still found a faint beat. "He's alive, Chuck. Bring me water. Quick."

He moistened the Indian's temples, forehead and lips, and after a few moments, his efforts were rewarded. The man's eyelids fluttered and slowly came open, his pupils lighting up with the spark of consciousness.

"Chuck, can you talk with him?"

"I know a little of their language. I'll try."

"See what you can find out."

Chuck bent down to the man and began to talk to him in guttural tones. Suddenly the man responded, barely whispering.

"What's he saying?"

"That he got shot in the spine and can't move any more. He also says that we saw his spirit, and thanks us for stopping."

"His spirit? I don't know whether to believe in those things, but may be there was something… Ask him who shot him."

Chuck translated, and the man answered.

"Who do you think, Reverend?"

"Bersa's guards?"

Chuck nodded.

"Ask him why."

Once more Chuck went to work in Falling Moon's tongue, and Falling Moon answered.

"He says he doesn't know why. There was no reason."

"None at all?"

"None at all. He and his braves were trapped by the guards and butchered down mercilessly though they had been promised a truce. Falling Moon was the only survivor, barely able to drag himself to this spot. He also said that the guards were looking for the two of us."

"Murderers!"

The Indian spoke again.

"He wants a favor."

"What favor?"

"He wants us to stay with him until he dies. He doesn't want to die alone."

Jeremy nodded affirmatively. "Get a blanket, Chuck."

They comforted the Indian to the extent possible, covering him and propping up his head, as well as moistening his lips with water. Falling Moon began to chant, the monotony of his voice lulling Jeremy and Chuck almost to sleep. But before that happened, there was silence, which alerted them to the fact that their friend had passed away. They quickly covered him with some stones, this being the only feasible manner of burial under the circumstances. As they got on their horses, Jeremy said, looking towards the mound, "I don't know your customs, but I pray that God has mercy on your soul."

Then he and Chuck rode off towards Jericho

+   +   +

"Well, Sheriff, what 'd you call us here for? We've been waiting for quite a spell now. Don't want to spend the whole night sitting around the jailhouse."

The one who spoke was Stovall, the banker; he wore a grey suit which matched his mustache and neatly-parted hair of the same color. With his ruddy cheeks and portly frame he was the very picture of a staunch supporter of the establishment. Right now his normally complacent features bore an annoyed expression.

"A little more patience, please," Earl Dugan begged. "One particular gentleman without whom we can't start the meeting is still missing."

"And who might that be? As far as I can see, all those who've got a say in Jericho are here." He motioned to the assembled.

Casting his eye over their round, Earl Dugan took inventory. Near the door, leaning against the adobe wall, was Derryl Adams, the storekeeper and erstwhile mayor, fiftyish, with the hanging jowls and the worried look of a blood-hound. Next to him was Bill Clark, the proprietor of the livery stable, a grizzled old-timer, whose twinkling eyes and sportily donned hat with its upturned brim belied his age. Farther around stood the blacksmith, Pete Thompson, a burly, square-shouldered giant, with a defiant jaw and a shiny bald head. On a stool sat Doc Browser, wearing a suit which had seen better days, a man with fine, intelligent features though evidently not of physical prowess. Reclining against the bars of an empty cell was Abe Hutchison, the carpenter and undertaker, who bore a serene expression, and who, had he worn a cassock, might have passed for a territorial judge. And in the cell itself, sitting on one of the cots was Johnny Shine, the barber, a sturdy young man with an impish face, who was still wearing his white smock. And of course there was also present the already mentioned Stovall and three other homesteaders who could be trusted. Yes, they were all there, all those Earl Dugan had invited the day before. A motley crew, to be sure. Would they be a match for Bersa?

Earl Dugan's gaze was met by Stovall's. "Well now, Sheriff. Who's the mystery man? And why can't we get started without him? If it's something that concerns our businesses, we want to know about it now. We have that right. Don't you agree, gentlemen?" He looked to the others for support, which he received to varying degrees. They nodded and mumbled yes.

Outside the Sheriff's office, two of Bersa's guards, were heading nonchalantly towards the Sheriff's office, where the meeting was taking place, each one with a bottle in his hand. Sally had stayed outside in the street together with her friend, Helen, the two serving as look-outs.

"We've got to do something about these two," Sally said. "We can't let them come in here. We have to distract them."

"We can invite them to my house," Helen suggested. "Fill them up with more drink until they pass out."

"That's a great idea. Let's do it." Addressing the approaching guards, she said, "Howdy, boys. What brings you here on this fine evening?"

The guards looked surprised, not having noticed the girls in the dark until now. They were pleased that they were from the opposite sex, and pretty and young to boot. "Evening, ladies. We came to check with the Sheriff to see how things are going."

"My dad is out," Sally said. "They called him from one of the ranches. An argument that turned out bad. He won't be back soon. You'd best come back later."

"What do you think, Abe," one of the guards, whose face featured a broken nose distinct even in the dark, said. Do you want to come back later?"

"No, Hank, " the other, a bulky wardrobe of a man, said. "I'd rather stay here. I like the company." He took a swig from his bottle.

"Me too, Abe. Let's have a party."

"If that's what you want," Helen cut in. "I've got the perfect place for it. At my house, just down the street. My folks won't mind. They're asleep. Nobody will bother us."

"You hear that Abe?" said the broken nose. "Nobody will bother us. How does that sound to you?"

"Sounds great," Hank said. "I'm out of booze as it is. Let's go." He threw away his empty bottle and slung his free arm around Helen, who did not resist and led the way towards her house. Hank, the wardrobe, did likewise with Sally after casting his own bottle aside, and they all moved down the street in a small caravan, both Crusaders unsteady on their feet and the girls propping them up.

Inside the Sheriff's office the discontent and impatience of the gathered was growing. Earl Dugan could feel the sweat condensing on his face. Where was the confounded preacher? He had to stall; he would give them something to ponder.

"Certainly you have a right to be informed, gentlemen," he said, "and you will be soon. But I'll have you know that there is much more at stake here than your businesses. I'm talking about survival – yours and mine and that of this town. It's a question of life and death, to put it plain, and I reckon with that much in the balance, you can postpone your poker games, or whatever else you have in mind, for a little while longer."

Taking advantage of the startled hush his words had produced, Earl Dugan was about to check in the living quarters next to his office to see whether perhaps Jeremy had arrived by that route, when the door flew open as if blown by the wind and the long-awaited young man entered from the street, followed by his friend, both of them looking ragged and weather-beaten.

"Sorry to have kept you waiting, gentlemen," Jeremy excused himself, tipping his hat. "I was held up by an unexpected matter. Tried to make it here as fast as I could."

Stunned, they all remained silent. Then someone exclaimed, "Cadoc!" Which set off an alarmed mumbling around the room, presently interrupted by the Sheriff.
"Yes, it's Cadoc," Earl Dugan affirmed, and addressed Jeremy, "Let me introduce these gents to you, Reverend." He went through their names one by one, concluding, "We can start the meeting now."

"Wait a minute!" Stovall had recovered the power of speech. "You mean to say he's the one we've been waiting for all evening? I don't see how he can be useful to us. He'll be lucky if he can save his own skin from Bersa. In fact, the best thing we can do is turn him in immediately."

Again a mumbling arose, and this time it was in support of Stovall, putting Earl Dugan on edge. He sensed that the crucial moment had arrived at which he had to bring into play whatever influence and powers of persuasion he possessed over these men, if he wanted to incline them towards Jeremy. Everything else depended on that.

The mumbling of those present grew louder.

"Hold it, boys," he said, straightening up a little more and sticking his thumbs in his belt. "I understand your feelings well. We're all in the same boat here. We're all under Bersa's whip – I as much as you. But now I ask you, do you want to go on like this until doomsday? Do you forever want to be slaves who work the seat off their brow for another, and who never have any say in their destiny?

Do you always want to cower in fear and bury your pride and manhood? Do you want to continue putting up with the rape of your women, the theft of your property and the repression of all your human rights? Do you want to live like animals with no end in sight?" He paused briefly, then continued. "For my part, I don't have the least desire, and if you share my feelings, I ask you to listen to this young man here. Give him a chance to explain himself – you've got nothing to lose by it. Lend him your ears, and it might change your lives."

Earl Dugan stepped back, surprised at his own impassioned oratory, which had flowed from his lips almost without his doing. He observed the reaction of those present. The latter looked at each other questioningly. Perhaps he had convinced them.

"Reckon you got a point, Sheriff," the blacksmith spoke up. "Let's hear Cadoc out. Ain't no harm in that."

"The others nodded in agreement. "All right, then. Let the preacher talk."

Animated, Jeremy stepped forward into their circle. "Friends," he began, pushing back his jacket and placing his hands on his hips. "Most of you have seen me only once before, and that was in church and under circumstances which did not permit me to meet each of you personally. Let me affirm to you once more now that I am a legitimate minister of the church who has been officially appointed to serve in your parish. Therefore my number one obligation is to you, my parishioners, whose well-being – both spiritual and physical – I must always have at heart; my second obligation is to my church, whose integrity I am bound to uphold. As we all know, both the rights of the parishioners as well as the principles and décor of the church have been severely compromised in this town, and I declare here and now that I myself shall remove the cause of the violations that have occurred. I pledge to you, my friends, that I shall remove Macum Bersa, a corrupt and criminal man – a plague to mankind."

More mumbling and questioning glances among the gathered.

"And how are you going to do that?" Adams, the storekeeper, asked skeptically.

"He'll preach him a sermon, like he does to us, and then he'll pray that Bersa will be a good boy and leave," Hutchison, the undertaker, suggested slyly.

There was some chuckling.

"He'll hex him," piped Shine, the barber. "The preachers have power over Satan himself and call him up when they need to. And what better remedy than to fight one devil with another!"

More laughter.

"Wrong on both counts," Jeremy said good-humoredly. "My plan is much more down-to-earth. Let me explain. As you know, this town will in a few days be subjected to the ultimate humiliation of being forced to celebrate Bersa's tenth anniversary in Jericho. What better occasion than that to organize an uprising against him and his gang? According to my information, Bersa and his guards will have a big orgy at the saloon. We can hit them late that night when they're drunk. With the support of all the men who live in this town we should be able to beat them."

Jeremy observed the gathered, waiting for their reaction. They seemed reluctant.

"What about guns?" the blacksmith asked. "We're not allowed to carry any on the day of the celebration. The guards are gonna check everybody."

"We can hide them some place beforehand – perhaps right here in the jailhouse. We can build up an arsenal, ready to be used at the right moment."

"And Bersa's security?" Adams, the storekeeper, wanted to know. "Bersa always keeps some of his men sober to keep watch outside the saloon."

"We'll find a way to get rid of them There's only a few of them, but there's a lot of us."

"And what about Bersa himself? How are we going to deal with him? He never celebrates in the barroom with the run of his men. He'll be in his private quarters upstairs, where he can protect himself as if it were a fortress. I know his apartment well 'cause I've had to go there a few times. Bersa's got a weak heart that gives him trouble now and then." The speaker was Doc Browser, who indeed had had occasion to visit the upper floor of the Paradise.

Jeremy smiled almost imperceptibly. "Leave Bersa to me. I myself am familiar with his quarters, and will make sure that we'll get our hands on him." He paused and then went on, "Well, gentlemen, what do you say? Are you with me?"

He could sense them sway in his direction now, and thought that he had already won the battle. But there was one objection from Stovall.

"If you ask me, Cadoc's plan is too risky," the banker said flatly. "How are we – peaceful folks who never touch a weapon – to stand up against these professionals?

They'll shoot us to pieces. I say we should vote against this. After all, the way things are , we don't have it so bad. We have roofs over our heads, we have enough to eat, and Bersa's Crusaders, while policing us, also give us protection. If our rebellion fails, we stand to lose everything. Reject Cadoc's plan! That's my advice, and believe me, it's excellent advice."

Jeremy could see them waver again, moved by Stovall's impressive words, which reminded them of the dangers inherent in an uprising. He didn't want to lose them and addressed them now with growing passion. "Listen to me well, gentlemen. Your friend Stovall here is right. If the rebellion gets crushed, you'll have to pay for it. Bersa will take bloody revenge – you can be sure of that. But, if you decide not to collaborate with me, do you really believe you'll fare any better?"

Someone tried to interrupt the speech, but Jeremy requested silence by raising his hand and continued.

"I only want to remind you of what happened to the parents of my friend Chuck here, and to all the other upright citizens of Jericho whom Bersa has abused. You don't pay your contributions and Bersa'll have you beaten up, you don't obey one of his rules and he'll have you whipped, you refuse him your daughter and he might have you killed – any provocation at all serves him as an excuse to give free rein to his violent impulses, and lately he doesn't even need to be provoked." Jeremy thought of Falling Moon and the treachery of which he became a victim. "If you ride out to the canyons south of here," he said emotionally, "You'll find an entire band of Apaches butchered like animals at Bersa's whim – shot to death for sport. Do you people want to end up the same way? If you have to die, isn't it better to do so fighting than waiting passively? Think about it ….." His voice rose to a climax. "Think about it and support what I have proposed. It can be your salvation. Together we can win."

Recovering his breath, his face burning, he stepped back to wait for the response of those present. He had done all he could. If he still hadn't won them over, there was nothing more he could do now.

Renewed mumbling on the part of them men.

"Let's take a vote," Earl Dugan said. "All those in favor of Cadoc's plan, raise your hands."

"Yes, support Reverend Cadoc's plan, " a female voice could be heard from the back of the crowd. "We, the women of Jericho, will help in this fight in any way we can." It was Sally Dugan, who had slipped in from the street during the last part of Jeremy's speech. She and Helen had dealt with the two Crusaders quickly, plying them with a few more drinks out on the porch of Helen's house, from a bottle that Helen had found in her kitchen, and then had sent the two men, who could barely still stand on their feet, back to the Paradise. After which she had rushed back here. She now stepped to the front of the circle of the assembled citizens to join Jeremy and her father, who had started counting the raised hands.

They voted overwhelmingly in favor, with the exception of Stovall, though finally he too went along with them grudgingly. After that they discussed the specifics of their plan – how they were going to inform all the inhabitants of Jericho, what weapons they were going to use and how they were going to bring them into town, where and when they were going to meet on the day of the festivities, and in what way they were going to proceed during the attack itself. Then, one by one, the members of the clan-destine council made their exit until only Jeremy, Chuck, the Sheriff and Sally were left in the combined office and jailroom.

"Well done," Earl Dugan praised Jeremy. "You made a fine speech, Reverend. You'd make a great politician."

"So would you, Sheriff. You spoke to them very el-oquently." Jeremy turned to Sally. "Thanks for the boost, Sally. Yes, we need you and the other women."

"I'm glad everything went well," said Chuck. "And now we need to rest, Reverend. You and I have to be out of here before sunrise."

They spent the remainder of the night in one of the cells, on the two cots that were there – a welcome treat after having had to sleep on the hard ground for several nights. Early in the morning, Sally prepared them a breakfast. Jere-my was happy to see her again and gave her a warm glance, which was returned with equal intensity. But Jeremy and Chuck had to leave, and there was no time for further ro-mance. Having packed up their supplies, they sneaked out of Jericho at the break of dawn. The rising sun found them out on the range, headed for the canyons, their mission accomplished.

+   +   +

The blow came seemingly out of nowhere, and so suddenly that Jeremy had no time to put up resistance, but stumbled and fell on his back, remaining stretched out on the ground, stunned. He shook his head, attempting to clear it. Who or what had struck him? Some animal that had entered the cave during their absence – a mountain lion perhaps? He could feel the blood seeping out of a corner of his mouth and licked it. Then he remembered the gun in his holster and drew it, but out of the depths of the cave floated a dark shadow, and the weapon was knocked out of his hand. Focusing his eyes, Jeremy found that standing before him was Polk.

"So we finally meet again, Preacher," Polk gloated. "I knew you were here, no matter how much Higgins dismissed my hunch. I can trust my feelings …. I see that my rifle didn't disappear just like that….." He was gazing past Jeremy towards the horse ouside the cave and the Winchester tied to the saddle. "Well now," he continued, "old Bersa will be mighty glad to get his long-lost assistant back. But first," he added with anticipatory relish, "first we'll have some fun. You owe me from the other day, remember, Reverend?" He pulled his knife and brandished it.

"I owe you nothing," Jeremy said. "What happened at the church wasn't my fault." He was hoping that Chuck would arrive soon from below, where he had been lagging to water his horse.

"Oh yes, you owe me, Reverend, you surely do. May be we can freshen up those pretty skin markings of yours. They look a mite faded."

Suddenly Jeremy saw the knife flash towards his face, and barely managed to duck to the side to avoid it. Again the blade came towards him, but by now he had managed to get a hold of one of Polk's legs, and jerking it, made the man lose his balance. Polk stumbled and struggled to get back on his feet, but Jeremy wouldn't let go and pulled him down farther. In a moment they were rolling on the ground, locked in mortal combat, spilling out of the cave into the open, where they continued to fight. Jeremy knew that he was stronger than the other – he had no trouble preventing Polk from getting him into a firm hold. But Polk, light of build, was quicker, and Jeremy found it difficult to pin him down in his turn. And of course, Polk was wielding the knife, and it was indeed the latter which finally won out. Suddenly Jeremy felt it cold and sharp against his throat. For an instant he was able to keep it away, pushing the hand that held it, but then he felt it pressing against his skin once more with disturbing insistence.

"The game's over, Preacher. I win," Polk hissed, his repulsive reptile face close to Jeremy's.

It seemed that only a miracle could save Jeremy. Owing to the blade, he was defenseless. The slightest movement on his part and he would cut himself. All he could do was claw the ground with his free hand, attempting to perhaps pull himself away from under the blade, a maneuver that was to no avail.

Polk, having entertained himself sufficiently, was ready for the death blow now – Jeremy saw an icy expression creep into his pupils, and he consigned himself into the hands of the Lord. Through Jeremy's mind passed all the things that human beings remember at the moment of imminent death, but foremost he thought of Sally. Then, unexpectedly, Polk gasped, and eyes bulging, he dropped the blade he had been holding against Jeremy's throat and slumped. Chuck had arrived just in time, coming up on Polk from behind and stabbing him fatally.

"Chuck, thank God, you saved my life," exclaimed Jeremy, pushing the dead Crusader off himself and getting up.

Chuck retrieved his knife and wiped it on the deceased's pants. "What are we going to do with him?" he asked. "Bury him?"

Jeremy thought for a moment as he finished dusting himself off. He was beyond administering Christian rites to those he had killed. Things had gone too far for that. "No, we won't bury him," he said to Chuck. "I've got a better idea."

"What, Reverend?"

"Let's find Polk's horse. It must be in the canyon. We'll take the cadaver down, and then we'll arrange a present for Bersa, a present he'll never forget, and early anniversary gift, a fitting commemoration of his ten years in Jericho.

And they prepared the macabre offering.

Chapter 8

The bullwhip cut across his back like a fiery iron, searing into his bare skin easily, shooting a hot pain through every one of his nerves, making him want to bunch up and crawl into his mother's womb for protection, but he wasn't able to. He was tied around the wrists and suspended from the post in the center of the courtyard. His knees and legs barely touched the ground, and all he could do was struggle upward, bracing himself for the next blow.

"What do you think of that, runt?" he heard the voice of Granville, the overseer, through the humming in his head. "You still believe it was worth your while taking them bales? Well, you're gonna have to pay for each and every one of them now."

Again the rawhide bit into him, but this time he had expected it and was able to maintain his presence of mind better than before.

"Go to hell, you damn bootlicker."

Granville was incensed. "What was that, boy? Not only did your daddy forget to teach you right from wrong; he didn't learn you any manners neither. But don't you worry none. I'll take care of that. We'll turn you into somebody decent yet."

Crack went the whip, slicing into him with redoubled force, making him cave forward, making him wail, making everything swim before his eyes, making him forget about himself. His arms, his back, his legs – his entire body – did not exist any longer. There was only the pain now, burning, sizzling, tingling, totally enveloping him as if he were submerged in a cauldron of fiery liquid. Instinctively he groped to get to the surface of the flaming element, to shake it off and escape the scalding current, but there was another explosion of the whip, and again he was engulfed by lava.

"Are you going to thieve again, boy? Are you going to make off with any more cotton in the future?" Granville's snarl reached what remained of his consciousness. "And are you aiming to call me more unbecoming names?"

But he didn't want to give in. Pain was all he had left, and he suddenly found that he could turn pain into an ally, into a protective weapon which could help him preserve what there was left of his spirit. Instead of trying to fight it, he simply had to accept it, collaborate with it, enjoy it. Every new crack of the whip could be considered another addition to the pleasurable surf in which he was wallowing, a further intensification of the thrill of speeding along on the brink of death, and every interruption of the rhythm of strokes an insufferable delay which cruelly suspended his enjoyment, his relish, his paradisiacal delectation.

"Answer me," Granville barked. "Are you going to repeat these things?"

Agony had fortified his spirit and now strengthened his voice. "Yes, I will repeat them," he heard himself screaming. "I will repeat them….I will….I will….I will…. I will…..Macum…..Macum…..Macum…." They were no longer his own vocal chords, nor Granville's; it was an anxious, soft voice, a female voice – his mother's? No, his mother had died long ago.

"Macum…..Wake up!"

Macum Bersa opened his eyes and found himself looking into those of Brandy."

"Are you all right, Macum? You were screaming as if someone was trying to kill you. Calm down. It's over."

Bersa pushed himself up on his elbows and glanced about the room, dimly brightened by the morning sun that penetrated through the heavy drapes. "Yes, sweetie, yes…..," he said, gradually regaining his sense of reality. "They tried to do away with me but I managed to survive. And I aim to go on living for a long time to come." He pulled Brandy close in order to kiss her. "Today's the big day," he said. "Today we're going to have ourselves a good time."

He let himself fall back on the bed, pulling the girl down with him, and caressing her lightly, thought about the celebration ahead. Macum Bersa Day! Ten years on top! He had made it. It was he who gave the orders now, he who meted out justice at will, he who lived in luxurious sur- roundings in the manner of a country squire, he who had his choice of paramours, he who took his liberty to exploit the general run of men – the 'trash' – it was no longer the plantation masters. Those had perishes long ago in the war between the states, had received what had been their due, making room for a new breed of enterprising individuals like himself. It was no longer wealth or social status that counted; it was ingenuity and the will to survive, especially out here in the West, where those other conditions had never existed in the first place.

It had been a good move that he had thrown in with old Monty after the nearly fatal beating at Cheswick Hall that day. His folks hadn't wanted him with them any longer even though he had stolen the cotton at least in part for them: his father, a drunkard laborer who had to compete with the black slaves for work, couldn't feed all the mouths in the family adequately; so he – young Macum – had wanted to help. But no, they didn't care to have anything more to do with him after the incident – didn't want to get in trouble with the folks in the 'Big House' up on the Cheswick, who controlled the town of Asheville. So they told him to get moving as soon as possible. And then fate brought him across the path of the Reverend Jacob W. Montgomery. He still remembered his appearance on that first occasion when he – a boy of fifteen – happened upon that personage on the outskirts of town. A trim, silvery-haired old man dressed in black except for a dapper vest of red satin, he had looked very striking as he stepped out of his covered wagon and asked the youthful vagrant what he could do for him. Monty had known at a glance what was going on, and had taken pity on him; he had told him to wait in the back of the revival tent until the meeting that was about to start was over. And young Macum had been watching him, and had found himself inspired by him, admiring the way he could sway the crowd; and when later, after the people had dispersed, Monty took him to his wagon and casually counted the bills and coins he had collected, Macum had been deeply impressed indeed.

When Monty asked him to be his assistant and travel with him, there was no objection or doubt on his part. And then young Macum got to see the South, every corner of it – from Shreveport to Savannah, from Louisville to New Orleans, from Memphis to Charlotte – and Monty had taught him the tricks of his trade: how to preach hellfire and brimstone, how to hook people, that is, how to entertain them, how to fire them up and sweep them along, and most important, how to separate them from their money. Often they had to make a quick escape from the authorities, for Monty's methods were not always commensurate with what could be expected from a minister of the Lord. Many were the widows who handed him their savings in return for the promise of matrimony, a promise which turned out to be empty the morning after it was made; even outright theft was not beyond Monty if and when the opportunity presented itself to abscond with something he fancied – he was partial to fine jewelry in particular. Finally the arm of justice caught up with them in a place called Chalybeate, and they threw Monty in jail. Bersa remembered him in his cell the day after his trial and conviction, a sorry-looking old man who, for some time, had been suffering from some sort of consumptive ailment compounded by alcoholism, and was coughing constantly. He had slipped him a bottle between the bars – the jailkeeper hadn't watched Macum very closely because he was just a kid.

"Take the wagon and go, boy," Monty had said. "I've taught you all I know. Make the best of it. I myself am never going to get out. They'll take me to the federal penitentiary in Nashville, and that'll be the end." Macum had tried to animate him. "Don't worry, I'll find a way." And the next day he'd tried to slip him a pistol, but they caught him at it and told him to leave now on the double if he didn't want to be thrown in jail too. And so he had finally left old Monty behind and set out to fend for himself.

In the beginning it had been rough going; after all, though some three or four years older than when he left home, he was still only a youth, and no matter how much he tried to mimic the manner and style of his mentor, his young age would shine through, and he generally would fail to convince people of his divine calling and of the necessity to follow him and leave their money in piles. But out of compassion, they did give him enough to get by. After that came the war, and with it a chance to grow and hone his skills. They inducted him into the ranks of the Confederate Army as a minister, and he had the opportunity to socialize with the officers as much as with the common soldiers. He got to know their ways, learned how to handle men firmly, how to organize them efficiently, and it contributed to the foundation he had received from old Monty. There was strength added to his voice, authority to his manner, method to his thinking, developments which were accompanied by an amazing physical growth. Soon he became well-known in his entire regiment – known as the Red Giant or Reverend Flaming Torch. He restricted himself only to legitimate preaching at this point, refining his oratorical skills as much as possible, content with the comforts and recognition his post afforded him; but when, towards the end of the war, battles began to be lost by his regiment and he and his comrades had to retreat with increasing haste, he did not hesitate to make use of his special privileges and go beyond what was proper for a minister of the church.

Abandoning his flock at Shilo, he made his way through the back country in the opposite direction of Sherman's advancing troops, appropriating for himself in the name of the Lord any means necessary to facilitate his rush to safety – horses, carriages, food, money. When the South finally laid down its weapons at Appotomax, he was already on the Texas borderline, prepared to go on west, but on hearing of the surrender and the end of the war, he turned back. He'd still had some doubts as to whether, in the future, he should dedicate himself to being an honest minister or not, but he was already accustomed to certain luxuries and temptations alien to religion. Just then he ran across a cleric considered almost a saint, but shabby look-ing, dressed in worn rags that were falling off his body, and that decided for him the path he – Macum – should take, a path that was not that cleric's. The time had come to bring all the knowledge and experience he had acquired over the years into play; it was time to cash in on the spoils. It was the plantation masters' turn to be exploited now, in addition to all those who would present themselves for easy picking.

On his way back to Tennessee, he recruited his small force, selecting its members from the pool of drifters – dis-charged soldiers and assorted footloose criminals – that were swarming about aimlessly. Polk in Lousiana, as he was just about to be strung up on a live oak in retribution for a casualty to his favorite pastime – knife play. He had liked the man's sleazy looks immediately when coming upon the scene, and had managed to persuade the lynching mob to let him live in the name of God and of mercy – a first test of his now perfected oratorical powers. And then he had bribed the jail guard to let Polk go, and with him Higgins, who was in the same cell for some act of brutality or other he had committed. A few days later they had been joined by Murdoch, a disenchanted Confederate officer on the run – he was still wearing his uniform coat, though without the stripes. They never found out what he was escaping from, but Bersa had known that it wasn't just the war, or else the man wouldn't have thrown in with them so easily. They met him one late afternoon in a saloon in Clinton, Mississippi, where they had stopped for the night – a man sitting by himself in the midst of a wild crowd of soldiers and prostitutes. Intrigued, Bersa had ambled over to him, struck up a conversation and invited him to come along with them – he liked the man's reserved, intelligent bearing; and Murdoch had agreed after briefly talking with Polk and Higgins. The three had been the nucleus of Bersa's private army, which, on reaching Tullahoma, had swollen to twelve, its recruits enlisted with the promise of riches.

He had it all planned out neatly. He, the preacher, would draw the crowds to the meetings, would enthrall them with his oratory, would whip them up against Lucifer, and in particular against the Yankee devil. At the right moment his boys would step in to reap the harvest, relieving everyone in the congregation of their valuables and making off with the horses of the assembled. That way, by moving about quickly from one place to another, they could add to their booty fast, yet escape the reach of justice, weak enough as it was in the aftermath of the war.

But before they could start their scam, he had an old score to settle. On the evening they arrived in Asheville, it had been raining, making the neglected grounds of the Cheswick look especially dreary. The slaves' cabins appeared abandoned, but there was a dim light in Granville, the overseer's, house, and Bersa had five of his men surround it, telling Murdoch and Higgins to go in, grab the owner and bring him outside. Together with the others, he walked up to the porch of the large, decaying mansion, and when the black house servant opened the portal, he barged in without further ado. Old man Cavanaugh – the patriarchal owner – and his wife were easy game. They were upstairs in their bedroom, and two shotgun blasts were enough to do away with them in the fraction of a moment, leaving them shredded in the soft down. There was more resistance on the part of their son, in adjacent quarters, who had jumped out of bed and placed himself protectively in front of his wife. In an instant he was reeling forward, Polk's blade in his chest, leaving his consort exposed. Bersa abandoned her, as well as the daughter of the house – a lovely girl of fifteen they had dragged out from somewhere – to his men. Much as he would have liked to have participated in that distraction, he had a more pressing matter to attend to. In a moment he was out in the courtyard, where they had dragged Granville. They had tied him to a pole – the same pole from which Bersa had been dangling that afternoon – only Granville was facing them. "Remember me?" Bersa had asked, shining the lantern on himself to make sure Granville got a good look. "Remember the red-haired kid and them bales of cotton?" And then he had lashed out at him, knowing no restraint, crisscrossing Granville's face and torso with bloody streaks, disfiguring his features, turning his eyes, nose and mouth into a bloody pulp. Granville had offered Bersa money ….property….all he owned… so that he would not kill him, Nevertheless, soon the man's head was dangling lifeless while Bersa kept on lashing out, re-living his own agony in this orgy of blood. They left Granville dead, along with all those in the house, including the women – once Bersa's men were finished with them. And before abandoning the site, they put the torch to all the buildings and structures. Bersa could still hear the gay crackling of the flames now as he was lying in bed.

His thirst for revenge stilled, he and his men had dedicated themselves to the pursuit of what was their grander aim – the acquisition of wealth. And his original plan had worked out well. They robbed one congregation here, another one there, changing locales from week to week, and in spite of the fact that eventually the word spread of their doings, and particularly of his role, he succeeded time and again in capturing new groups of faithful in his net of persuasion. He found that people trusted him, that they were strangely attracted to him, be it because of his exotic appearance – he had let his flaming hair and beard grow long – be it because of some inherent charisma which had finally come into its own. And Bersa and his boys had grown richer. Now and then they raided a plantation and thus augmented their wealth, some of which was saved, but most of which was spent on pleasures of the moment. But at last the law, now represented by the military courts of the Yankees, began to catch up with them, just as it had with old Monty years before, and he didn't want to suffer the same fate.

So they had decided to head out west, starting their trek somewhat listlessly at first, roaming through Missouri,

Kansas, Arkansas, Oklahoma, the cowtowns of Texas and New Mexico, until finally someone had told them about Jericho. Going by the rumors, it seemed the ideal place to settle down – an isolated yet prosperous community of mostly homesteaders in a fertile hollow, an oasis in the Southwestern wasteland – and when they arrived, they found that indeed it lived up to their expectations. There was a church – little more than a dilapidated one-room shack – but there was no preacher: the last one had died a year before of some unidentified disease. So all Bersa had to do was jump into the gap. Soon he had the parishioners eating out of his hand. Initially Bersa took care to behave like an authentic minister, and before long the parishioners obeyed him, and grateful for his presence, as well as transported by his weekly sermons, did everything they could to please him: they restored and expanded the church under his guidance, transforming it into the substantial structure that it was now, in addition providing quarters for him and for his men; they paid him and his men a salary and gave them a privileged position in the social life of Jericho.

From there it was just another small step to what amounted to a complete take-over of the town. Bersa and his men led a life that was gradually more and more licentious. Bersa began exacting higher tithes with the pretext of wanting money for a variety of civic projects, then went on to establish himself in the saloon, supposedly because of the larger space and as a measure of moral purification, and he brought his boys into prominence, declaring them a kind of holy police force whose function it was to protect the town. To top it all off, he had finally received official recognition from the hierarchy of the Methodist Church.

Good preachers were hard to come by, and the elders back east were apparently glad that a capable person had taken over the reins in Jericho and they didn't have to search any further to fill the post. They had sent him his official letter of appointment by mail, no questions asked, and he had been ever since a legitimate minister of the Methodist Church. After that, he and the boys had led the good life, permitting themselves any luxury they fancied – women, food, drink, fine suits, weapons, horses, and in his case, exquisite artwork which he had brought in from the East at great expense, as well as certain exotic pleasures requiring unusual paraphernalia and décor; for the latter, Bersa had even hired special carpenters from other parts, who transformed the saloon according to his specifications, converting it into a fortress dedicated to his private tastes. Yes, they had led the good life, and with the exception of a few minor incidents, easily handled by the guards, they had done so undisturbed for an entire decade, maintaining their stranglehold on Jericho successfully. But now that he and his men at last seemed to have achieved all their aspirations, a genuine threat was presenting itself to their cozy existence. Cadoc! At a certain moment, not too long ago, they had begun to send him formally-schooled assistants from back east. The first one, McLoughlin, had been easy enough to handle, but this one was a tough nut to crack. Murdoch and his boys seemed to be unable to lay their hands on him. The fact that, while searching the canyons, they had done away with a bunch of redskins was small consolation. Bersa harbored a dislike for Indians, perhaps because they reminded him so much of what he himself used to be – a pariah at the lowest end of the scale. But whatever pleasure he had derived from Murdoch's exploit had been destroyed the next day by the arrival of Polk's cadaver, securely tied to his horse, which somehow had found its way into town from the desert. It was a grim reminder of Cadoc's enduring presence in the area. If he had killed Polk, whose turn was it next? No longer was it a matter of losing one of the less important members of the gang – one of those who had joined more recently; Cadoc had touched on the original core – a disturbing thought indeed. Bersa should have gotten rid of the rebellious assistant when he had had the chance to. Instead, foolishly, he had entertained a soft spot, recognizing in him something of himself when a youth – the same unbendable defiance – and because of that he had been able to escape.

But how had Cadoc succeeded in doing it? How could he have vanished that night without the guards, in front of his room, noticing anything? Bersa had his suspicions – suspicions which had grown since Cadoc had been reported going about with the Harrison boy, and since proof had been found that the Harrison place had been the young preacher's hideout. But Bersa wanted to make sure.

"Brandy, honey," he said with deceptive tenderness to the girl, whose head was resting on his chest.

She stirred sleepily "Yes, Macum…"

"Brandy, I want you to know something."

She yawned and raised her head, her dark eyes finding his. "What is it, Macum?"

He looked at her detached but curious – a scientist about to set in motion his experiment. "Brandy, I've got something to tell you concerning your folks."

"My folks?"

"Yes, they're dead"

"What?"

"They're dead," Bersa repeated without emotion. "I ordered them to be killed and had their place destroyed. There's nothing left."

Brandy suddenly became agitated and her hands clawed Bersa's shirt. "What are you saying, Macum? Are you playing with me? Is this a joke?"

"No, I'm serious. Murdoch took care of the matter. He personally killed your parents and set fire to the place. It burned all the way to the ground."

"But why, Macum? No, I don't believe you! It can't be true. You promised me you wouldn't touch them, ever – that you weren't going to harm them. You're joking – tell me you're joking."

But Bersa was relentless. "I wouldn't have done anything to them, but they caused me problems, and I couldn't overlook that. You remember Cadoc?" He saw her freeze. "Your folks helped him, and now he's creating difficulties – more than I need. You see why I had to do it." He pushed her off himself and watched her collapse into the pillows next to him, screaming convulsively. But he hadn't finished yet. "Which brings me to another matter….I've been asking myself something …You want to know what?"

Brandy continued lamenting without paying attention to him.

"Well, let me tell you. I've been wondering, for one thing, how Cadoc managed to escape from here that night, and for another, why he went to your folks for help – why to them and not someone else? Can you explain that to me?" Disregarding her hysteria, he grasped her hard by the jaw, pulling her head up. "Are you going to answer me?" he bellowed. "It was you, wasn't it? It was you who helped him. You broke my trust, didn't you?"

The girl seemed in a state of shock, but suddenly she became animated and struggled out of his grip, retreating to her side of the bed. "Yes, I did," she cried, glaring at him fiercely. I did break your trust. And why not? Haven't you done the same to me? I gave you loyalty, and what did I get in return? Nothing. You've been carrying on with one after another of those sluts that you brought from other places. I tried not to let it bother me, thinking that in the end you'd always come back to me. But it's obvious that things have changed. You're spending too much time with that other one – Charysse – doing ugly things that I don't like. And me you want to throw away like an old rag. You're a bastard, Macum. I hope you die, you son-of-a-bitch, I hope you die soon….."

Bersa looked at her coldly. "Your time's run out," he said under his breath. "I've got no more use for you." There was a knock on the door, and he got up, throwing on his robe.

"Is everything all right, Reverend? I heard screams and wanted to see if there was some problem. Pardon the interruption."

It was Higgins – precisely the right man for the occasion. Bersa had heard about Higgins' sadistic tastes long ago, information again confirmed by Murdoch recently. Now these tastes would come in quite handy.

"No, you're not interrupting, Higgins. You're just the man I need. I know you appreciate a pretty lass when you see one, and I've got a real treat for you. You see Brandy, here? I'm through with her. Do with her whatever you like. You have my permission."

Higgins beamed with happiness. "Thanks for the present, Reverend." And he eagerly approached the bedstead, stalking the distraught girl, who backed away from him until the headboard got in her way, and then he threw himself at her, letting out a savage roar.

Bersa left the room, entering an adjacent one to attend to his hygiene. He had to get ready for church service at noon and for the homage they were to pay him. It had been all over with Brandy at any rate; the girl had shown him much affection during their relationship, but underneath the surface she always seemed to have harbored resentment, seemed to have scorned him. He was tired of her, and besides, he already had a replacement. Higgins will take good care of her, he thought, filling the washbowl with water from the pitcher in order to proceed with his ablutions.

Suddenly he felt a pressure on his heart, a tightness which took away his breath. Another seizure? Luckily the medicine was within his reach. He opened a cabinet, and groping around for a moment, produced a flask and a spoon, onto which he measured a few drops. Almost as soon as he had swallowed them, the weight on his chest got lighter, and he could breathe more easily and felt considerably better. Only a mild one, but a source of concern! The last time this had happened, Doc Browser had said that it was a highly unusual phenomenon in a man his age, and that it probably wouldn't occur again in many years, but now it had just hit him once more. Too many upsetting things had been happening lately – that probably accounted for it, as much as all the high living he had permitted himself. He would have to carry the medicine around with him just in case, and would have to call in the Doc again, and what was most important, hw would have to get rid of the principal cause of these disturbances which seemed to aggravate his condition and bring on the attacks. In one way or another, he would have to deal with Cadoc definitively, either by apprehending him or keeping him out of Jericho for good. But today was his day of honor, and he would try not to let problems of any sort spoil his enjoyment. Thinking thus, he began to wash himself, daydreaming about the festivities that were being prepared, and the special pleasures he had lined up for himself that evening.

Chapter 9

When Bersa entered the vestry, the Sheriff was already waiting for him, together with Murdoch and some other guards.

"Everything set, Dugan?"

"Yes, Reverend. They're all assembled – the whole community of Jericho – prepared to do you the honors."

"Then what are we waiting for? Go on, Dugan. Announce my arrival."

The Sheriff left through the door that led to the principal nave of the church, and Bersa sat down, tossing his gloves on the table.

"Well. What do you think, Murdoch? Will everything go all right today?"

"Rest easy, Reverend. We've got everything under control. There have never been any problems during past celebrations; so why should there be any now? Me and the boys checked everybody and made sure nobody's carrying arms. Besides, if I do say so, the folks in town appear to be truly happy. I've never seen them happy like this, except during the early days, when we first got here. Could be that, after all, they appreciate all the nice things we've done for them." He laughed cynically.

"And Cadoc? Is he going to bother us?"

"How can you think that!" Murdoch seemed almost offended. "There's no way he'll bother us. We've got Crusaders everywhere. There's no way Cadoc can enter Jericho, let alone get through to where you are. Relax, Reverend, and enjoy yourself. Enjoy the treats the fine people of this town have prepared for you. We'll take care of the rest."

But Murdoch's assurances failed to put Bersa completely at ease. He could not shake off the image of Polk and his stiff cadaver, out of which the buzzards had already torn strips of flesh. It stayed with him, firmly imprinted in his mind; it stayed with him as, beckoned by one of the guards who had been watching the congregation through one of the cracks, he got up and walked out in front of the altar to greet the assembled, as he graciously received their standing ovation, as he listened to a speech by Earl Dugan praising him and his civic achievements, as he accepted an engraved gold plaque naming him the most distinguished citizen of Jericho. It continued to be on his mind during his own speech of gratitude and the following brief service delivered by himself, during the ensuing parade from the church into town, formed by the gaily-decorated buckboards of the people of Jericho and concluded by his own coach, during his arrival at the Paradise, in front of which a crowd had gathered in order to cheer and set off firecrackers, and while passing through the barroom, where he received another noisy ovation from the guards gathered there. Even when he finally was in his apartment on the upper floor to be the object of a toast and have dinner with his closest associates, did Polk's gruesome image remain with him. Only when he thought of the special private entertainment that would crown the occasion for him later that night, was he able to push it out of his mind. Charysse knew her business well – it would be an insuperable experience, a divine thrill indeed. To re-live the punishment that day in the courtyard of the Cheswick was the only way in which he could truly savor his success, in which he could ultimately overcome the past, in which he could at last feel on top, and indeed, it would form a prodigious culmination of Macum Bersa Day.

+   +   +

The door creaked lightly as if someone were trying to steal in, and Jeremy drew his gun, getting up abruptly from his chair and posting himself behind the door. But it was only Sally Dugan.

"I didn't want to alarm you, Reverend. I thought you were asleep on the bed. Just wanted to see whether you needed something."

He stashed the gun back in the holster. "Thank you, Sally. I'm fine. I've been sitting here in the chair, thinking….."

"Thinking about what, Reverend?"

"Thinking about tonight's plans…..How are things outside? Are they whooping it up? I heard fireworks."

"They're celebrating a lot – Macum Bersa and his cutthroats in the saloon, and us ordinary folks under the open sky, out in the streets, thinking about how we'll be rid of them soon. Old man Rufus McBride is playing the fiddle and has got everybody jumping. It's a shame that you can't be out there with us." Her face looked animated and especially pretty, framed as it was by her carefully arranged golden locks; her trim virginal shapes were highlighted by a simple pink dress.

"I don't know how to dance, Sally. That's one thing they didn't teach me in Bible School. But if I did, I'd consider it a great honor to be able to take a turn with you."

She blushed. Then closing the door behind herself, she stepped farther into the room. "There's something I've been wanting to tell you, Reverend…."

"What, Sally?"

"It's not very easy to express, because it concerns my Pa," she began insecurely. "My Pa's sick, Reverend. He's been drinking for a long time, and I've seen him sliding down. I shouldn't make any excuses for him, but my Ma died tragically, and that was what got him started. That crushed him, and then Bersa destroyed what was left of his spirit." She had started to sob, and paused to wipe her tears with a handkerchief. "At any rate," she went on, "what I wanted to tell you was that I'm extremely grateful for all you've done for him. During the last few days, since he started working on the project against Bersa, he's changed. He's been drinking less and has recovered some of his self-respect. He's almost become the confident man again that he once used to be. The talk he gave to the townsfolk the other night at the gathering made me feel good. And if we succeed in delivering Jericho from that plague of criminals, then my Pa will be completely himself again – a father whom a daughter can be proud of. I'm grateful to you, Reverend. If it weren't for you, this would never have been possible."

Her tears were flowing freely now, and Jeremy felt an impulse to console her.

"Calm down, Sally, please….." he grasped her gently by the shoulders to steady her and suddenly felt her leaning against him, burying her head in his chest. He felt her warm breath, her trembling body, and smelled the fine scent of her hair, and he himself began to lose control. "Don't worry, Sally. Everything will be all right," he said trying to dominate his own emotions as the girl continued to press herself against him; he raised up her face, and then, suddenly, he no longer had the strength to repress his instincts and let his lips find hers.

They kissed with urgency, embracing each other unrestrained, losing any notion of time and place, allowing themselves to be swept away by their feelings. Feverishly he unbuttoned her dress. He didn't have much experience in matters of the flesh, but what he lacked in practical knowledge he made up for with passion. Soon their bodies were entwined in bed, and all the anxieties and tensions of the past week were forgotten. Afterwards they lay in silence, and the whole enormity of what had just occurred hit Jeremy's conscience. He felt guilty that as a man of the cloth he had taken advantage of this innocent creature when that was prohibited by society's and the church's rules and conventions. For a moment he felt more sinful and evil than Bersa himself. But there was no use in beating himself up; his feelings had been sincere, and there was only one way to rectify things.

"I love you, Sally, " Jeremy said. "When this is all over, I want to marry you."

"And I love you and want to marry you too. I knew it from the moment I saw you."

He held her tight. "As soon as we get a chance, we'll speak with your Pa."

There was a knock on the door, and the two love birds jumped up and hastily put on their clothes and straightened out the bed so that nobody would suspect anything.

"Are you awake, Reverend?"

"Of course, Sheriff. Come in."

Earl Dugan entered and, noticing his daughter, directed a curious look at her, then another at Jeremy, but he said nothing.

"Sally's been telling me what's happening in town," said Jeremy. "I hope our people aren't overdoing the celebrating."

"They're only passing the time, waiting for us to give them the word. Everything's set and ready. All the men are there, and we've got plenty of guns in the back of Johnny Shine's shop. The only thing holding us back is Bersa's guards, who are prowling the streets."

"We have to wait until they disappear after dark," Jeremy said. "Only then can we attack." He thought of Macum Bersa and that night that he had observed him in his special chamber, doing penitence. "Only then, at a certain hour, will everything be in our favor, and only then will we be successful. But," he went on, "let me wake up Chuck. The fellow hasn't opened his eyes ever since we got here last night."

He signaled Sally and her father to leave the room ahead of himself, and followed them in order to find his companion, who was profoundly asleep in an adjacent room, in order to get him ready for the attack on the saloon.

+   +   +

They had picked the barbershop as their arsenal because it was less conspicuous than the jailhouse. It was more natural for a large number of men to pass through its doors in broad daylight. Nobody thought anything of it. Besides, the barbershop had a convenient storeroom in the back – large enough to hide the assortment of weapons they needed to arm the force they had enlisted for their cause: practically all the able-bodied men in the Jericho area.

Jeremy sized them up by the amber glow of a lantern as they filed in one by one out of the dark and were handed their guns by Earl Dugan. None of them looked very strong, with lean frames and haggard faces – hardworking farmers and townspeople: but their strength resided in their aggregate number rather than in their individual physical capacity. There were more than two score of them, including the members of the council, and if he remembered right, there were only some twenty of Bersa's Crusaders left. Even if the guards were better shots, the rebels had a good chance to crush them, especially if the Crusaders were drunk. And of course they had one advantage Bersa did not possess – their will to survive, their determination to fight for what was theirs. And that was perhaps the factor Jeremy trusted in most.

"Is everybody here?" Jeremy asked Earl Dugan, who had finished handing out the guns.

"I think so, Reverend. We can get going as soon as you give the word."

Jeremy knew that the right moment was not far off. When, together with Chuck he had stolen across from the jailhouse to the barbershop, everything had already been quiet in town, excluding the noise of the guards at the saloon which was filling the night. They had to be fairly drunk by now. And Bersa was probably occupied with his private delights. "Send out someone to see how many Crusaders are keeping watch outside the saloon," he said. "Then we'll get on with it."

They sent Shine, the barber, who returned after a few minutes. "There's three in front of the building, and two in back," he announced. "The others are inside drinking."

Earl Dugan looked to Jeremy. "What's the plan?"

Jeremy thought briefly. "Chuck and I are going to take care of the guards outside – first the three at the door, then the two in back. Once that's done, we'll surround the building with all the men we have, and give an ultimatum to those that are inside. If they don't respond, we'll charge…. How does that sound, Sheriff?"

"Sounds fine to me. I'll explain it to the others." He communicated the plan to the assembled, who had been conversing in low tones, and addressed in particular the members of the municipal council, each of whom had been put in charge of a portion of the farmers and townsmen. "Adams, Thompson, Doc, Hutchison – you cover the front and storm the saloon from there if necessary. Stovall, Shine and Clark, you cover the back; make sure that nobody escapes by that route. Shoot down any of the gang that come in your way….Any questions?"

"Yes," said Doc Browser. "Are we to take prisoners?"

"Only if they give themselves up immediately. Otherwise it's not worth taking unnecessary risks…..More questions?

"I've got one regarding Cadoc," Stovall said. "Exactly what role is the Reverend going to play during all this? Is he going to fight with the rest of us?"

"Don't worry about him. He has special responsibilities during the attack in order to make sure that nobody escapes. Of course he's going to fight with us."

The banker didn't seem very satisfied, but Earl Dugan did not pay him any further attention. Instead he approached Jeremy, who was waiting on the side.

"We're ready, Reverend?"

"Good. May the Lord be on our side. Let's go," Jeremy said. He grasped the shotgun with which he had armed himself and motioned to Chuck. The two left the barbershop, followed by the others, and advanced stealthily through the darkness towards the cantina. They arrived without mishap, waiting in the shadows of the adjacent building. They could see the three guards, reported by Shine, on the porch: one of them was leaning back in a chair, with his feet on the banister, rolling a cigarette by hand, another was leaning against a pillar that held up the roof, humming a simple tune, and the third was bending over a watering trough in the street, refreshing his face. The three seemed wasted, having done their share of celebrating, and the one by the trough, in fact appeared to be swaying on his feet.

Jeremy made a signal to Earl Dugan, indicating that he and the others should wait; then he addressed Chuck. "I'll take care of this one first," he said with reference to the guard who was washing himself. "Then we'll deal with the ones on the porch."

Chuck nodded and pulled his bowie.

The two approached closer, their footsteps getting lost in the din that came out of the saloon. Jeremy, without trouble, managed to reach the one by the water trough, who was still dousing himself, and suddenly pushed his head under the surface completely; the man struggled, but Jeremy kept his head submerged until he stopped moving. Only then did he release him, dropping his limp body and then crouching behind the trough and waiting. Out of force of habit, he said a silent prayer for the man's soul, knowing that this killing had been for survival, as had been the previous two he had committed to date. How many more were there to come? He did not have time to think about it.

"Hey, Smitty," one of those who were on the porch, said. "What's the matter? Did you pass out?..... He's totally smashed. Go help him Johnny."

There were footsteps on creaking boards, then in the dust of the street. Jeremy, behind the trough, suddenly saw the one named Johnny appear and stood up quickly. With the shotgun he was carrying he gave the guard a blow on the head, which caused him to collapse. Turning to the porch, he saw the guard in the chair collapse as well, falling forward, losing his hand-rolled cigarette and his hat. The chair, upon falling down, rumbled, and both Jeremy as well as Chuck, who was pulling his knife from the guard's corpse, held their breaths for a moment. But those who were in the interior of the saloon did not seem to have heard anything.

Jeremy motioned to Earl Dugan to approach with those who were waiting; then, together with Chuck, he went to the back part of the building in order to render the guards there useless. Just as the ones in front, these men seemed victims of the occasion – one of them was even snoring – and Jeremy and Chuck had no problem putting them out of combat by means of a few quick blows. Again

Jeremy signaled, and soon Stovall, Shine and old man Clark appeared together with several other men in order to take their positions. Jeremy showed them the door through which he had made his escape with Brandy's help.

"Watch it closely. Don't let anybody who comes out get away. Later Chuck and I will return, and we'll take it by force – all of us together."

Stovall seemed bothered. "What's so important about this door? Who's going to come out of there?"

"Bersa himself, possibly. It's a secret exit from his private apartment. I know this part of the saloon interior well; that's why I want to participate in the assault personally. Is that clear?"

The men indicated their conformity.

"Very well. I'll take two of you with me and we'll see each other in a while. And if there's shooting, don't lose your heads."

Accompanied by Chuck and two men selected from the group, Jeremy continued circling the building, stationing the pair on the side that was not yet covered, where there were some windows. Then he and young Harrison completed the circle, arriving at the saloon entrance, where they encountered Earl Dugan and the men assigned to him – all of them positioned for the attack. Thompson stood by the swing door; Hutchison, Adams and the Doc manned the windows, and the remaining men were distributed on the porch and on the stairs that led up from the street.

"Well, Sheriff," Jeremy said, casting a glance at the interior of the saloon through the door, "let's end this party with a culminating attraction." He addressed two homesteaders, pointing to the Crusader named Johnny on the ground near the trough, who was stirring. "Splash some water in his face, and then bring him to me."

The two men did as asked, dragging the still dazed guard, whose head was blood-smeared, towards Jeremy.

The young minister stuck his shotgun into the man's ribs. "Take a good look around and count how many we are….Now go in the saloon and tell your friends. Tell them that they must surrender. If not, we're going to kill them all. As you can see, you don't have the slightest chance to escape. Go on. Move." He pushed the man with the barrel, and bewildered, the Crusader stumbled up the steps. Then Jeremy gave him one last big shove that sent him flying through the swing door into the bright turbulence of the saloon; after which Jeremy quickly stepped aside.

Inside the barroom, the clanging of the honky-tonk gave way to the hysterical shrieking of the girls and the startled grunting of the men. Then the voices died down and an eerie hush fell over the establishment.

"Give yourselves up, Crusaders," Jeremy bellowed. "And tell your boss to do the same. You're completely surrounded. There's no hope for you."

There was no response from inside, although some discussion in a low voice could be heard.

"Give yourselves up," Jeremy repeated. "Throw out your weapons and come through the door one by one if you want to avoid bloodshed."

There was still no answer. But then Murdoch's voice rang out. "Hey, Dugan. I want to talk with you – not with that two-bit preacher. Tell me – what's happening? Have all of you lost your senses? You really think you can threaten us – the Crusaders? Do you realize what will happen if we find ourselves obliged to fight our way out of here? I won't go into the details, but I swear it's not going to be a picnic. So stop that nonsense. You, Dugan, have them lay off that stupidity. If not, you're going to regret it, believe me."

"Not a chance, Murdoch," the Sheriff answered firmly. "This time we're not going to follow your orders. We don't have to. We're strong enough to lick you and all your men, and what's more, we have the firm will to do it. I advise you to do what the Reverend said. Throw out your weapons and march out one by one. It's your only chance to save your skins."

There was loud laughter in the interior. "Hey, preacher," Murdoch shouted. "How much are they paying you for organizing this little show? …For I can't believe that these numbskulls have put it together themselves. How much, eh? Whatever the amount, we'll double it. Is it a deal? Or are you doing all this just to serve God Almighty?" He emphasized the last words sarcastically, and his companions roared again; but when Jeremy didn't answer, Murdoch got serious. "Well, have it your way, then. But if you want us, you'll have to come and get us. You think you have the *cojones* to do it? We'll give you a warm reception, you can be sure of that." More laughter, underlined by the crack of a gun and a bullet that came whistling through the swing door.

Jeremy ran out of patience. "Go to the devil, all of you," he exclaimed, sticking the shotgun over one of the door flaps and finding a target. And that was the beginning.

The first blast ripped a corner out of a table, taking with it half the face of the guard ducking behind it. The second blast felled two other men, hitting one of them in the abdomen as he stood there, legs spread, firing his revolver, the other in the neck and chest as he was kneeling behind a chair, taking aim over the backrest. Further Crusaders were slaughtered by the rounds of Jeremy's companions, who began to fire through the windows and, standing next to him, through the entrance.

"Forward, friends. Let's go," Jeremy shouted and flung himself through the swing door, rolling on the floor until he reached a side-ended table which he could use for cover. He drew his Colt and fired at one of the guards, who was aiming at him from the bar counter, puncturing the man's forehead, then another one, smashing his eye, then dispatching two more bullets which shattered the glasses on the wall behind the bar.

The others had entered behind him: Chuck was putting his Colt to good use from behind another side-ended table on Jeremy's right, further over were Dugan and Thompson with the men under their command, while on the left Hutchison, Adams and the Doc had spread out with their men, using assorted pieces of crippled furniture for protection, or simply flattening themselves on the floor.

If they had thought they could simply overrun the Crusaders and mob them by sheer force of number, they were mistaken, Jeremy realized. Seasoned gunfighters, Bersa's men had taken advantage of any solid structure that existed in the saloon interior. A number of them had hidden behind the bar, others behind the massive piano, and still others were firing from the balcony at the top of the broad staircase, securely protected by the massive pillars that rose to the high ceiling. As a result, the invasion of the townsmen had come to a quick standstill after the first surge into the saloon; in fact, the intruders were in danger of being repelled, since they were much more exposed than the guards, who were firing well-aimed rounds unhurriedly now. Reviewing the scene, Jeremy could see several of his comrades-in-arms injured by the bullets: Adams bled from the temple, the Doc was holding on to his thigh, and several other men were writhing in Pain. The young minister knew he had to take quick action.

He motioned towards Chuck and Thompson. "Come with me. Let's take the piano." Then he turned to Earl Dugan. "Sheriff, you cover us."

Led by Jeremy, they advanced towards the mauled instrument, which was no longer playing a happy tune but was wailing off-key in the throes of annihilation while a barrage of gunfire from their companions in the rear guard held off the Crusaders entrenched in different spots. To turn the piano around when they reached it was a maneuver easily achieved through the agency of the gigantic blacksmith. Caught by surprise, the four guards behind it were unable to react to their attackers with sufficient speed, and Jeremy and Chuck dispatched them quickly and efficiently. Then, with the help of the blacksmith and some of the other townsmen, they pushed the piano towards the bar, employing it at the same time as a cover against those on the balcony. Once the ponderous instrument came to a standstill against the bar, the only thing left to do was to come out in the open and jump over the top, which they proceeded to do. Jeremy was deposited practically into the lap of one of Bersa's men, whose jaw he smashed with his elbow, knocking him out cold. Snatching the pistol from the man's limp hand, he fired at the other guards cowering there, helped by Chuck and a wiry homesteader whose face glowed with satisfaction as he let the barrel of his six gun smoke. Within a few moments they had eliminated all resistance in this fortified corner, leaving five of the Crusaders dead; then they directed their efforts to the balcony.

All the other townsmen, including the Sheriff, Hutchison, Adams and even the Doc – in spite of his leg wound – had advanced farther, controlling most of the saloon now; and Thompson was still behind the piano, firing shots. It would be only a question of time, Jeremy calculated, until they'd take the upper floor; there were only seven or eight Crusaders left. He checked the balcony, when suddenly he saw a stealthy movement – a shadow slinking towards Bersa's apartment, then another: Murdoch and Higgins. He fired two shots but apparently missed, and the figures disappeared through a door. He thought about the Paradise's rear exit door. In the heat of battle he had forgotten about it; he had better go there now before the pigeons flew the coop. Here in the saloon he was no longer needed; Dugan and the others could mop up by themselves. Having re-loaded his gun, he motioned to Chuck. "Let's go. We have some business to take care of." They withdrew easily from the saloon while the townsmen held those on the balcony at bay, and once outside, rushed to the rear part of the building.

But it was too late. There was Bersa, already mounted on a horse, his blond mistress, Charysse, on another, and surrounding them, Murdoch, Higgins and three other Crusaders, whose guns were blazing in response to the ineffective shots fired by the townsmen responsible for watching this part of the building. They took off at a gallop and in an instant were already out of reach of the townsmen's weapons, disappearing into the night.

Jeremy was furious. "Stovall, Clark, Shine, how could you let this happen? Why didn't you stop them?"

Stovall was apologetic. "Sorry, Reverend, but they burst out so suddenly, guns spitting bullets, that we were taken by surprise. Shine and his men were checking one side of the building, and Clark with his men the other. Neither one of them could get here fast enough when the mayhem started. Me and my boys, we simply couldn't handle them alone. Their horses were brought – I don't know from where – and before we knew it, the gang was mounted. Sorry again, Reverend."

"Well. There's nothing we can do about it now. They got away, and we have to wait till morning to look for them. For the moment, let's check what's left in Bersa's private chambers. Follow me."

They entered through the back door, open now, and trampled up the stairs one after another, Jeremy in the lead, Chuck behind him, followed by the rest. Walking down the corridor through which he had escaped with Brandy's help, they opened each one of the rooms they passed and in several found evidence of a wild bacchanalia – the remains of food and drink, women's attire carelessly strewn about – but there was no sign of any guard or any other living being. But finally, when they arrived at Bersa's principal bedroom – the same one in which he had invited Jeremy to participate in the private orgy that first night – they did notice a human being, someone apparently asleep on the gigantic mattress, though, under the circumstances, it had to be a strangely fast sleeper; sporadic shots could still be heard from the barroom. Then Jeremy realized that it was a girl, a girl wearing a lacey nightgown, a girl with dark hair – the back of her head was twisted toward him in a strange twisted manner, even though her body was frontally exposed. When he touched her head and delicately brought her face around, there was no longer any doubt about the girl's identity.

"My God," he whispered, and then turning to Chuck, "Don't come near, Chuck. Don't come near…"

But Chuck had already seen and grew pale. "Brandy!" he exclaimed. "What 'd they do to you?" He hugged her disconsolately.

Jeremy, grasping him gently by the shoulders, pulled him back after a moment and steered him towards the door, intending to remove him from the scene of his sister's murder. Chuck was like a sack; he allowed himself to be guided without resistance, his spirit broken, but suddenly Jeremy could feel his body become heavy, and he slid from his grip. Before he could avoid it, his friend had collapsed on the floor.

"Chuck!"

Bending down to check him, Jeremy found him unconscious. At first he thought that it was due to the emotional shock he had just received, but then he noticed a large stain on Chuck's shirt, near the beltline, and then, lifting up the fabric, he saw blood oozing out of the nasty opening which a bullet had ripped into his torso.

"Get Doc Browser so this man won't die!" he shouted to those who had arrived in the meantime. And he took one of the blankets off Bersa's bed to cover him.

Then he fell into a chair, overcome by fatigue. At that moment Sally arrived and proceeded to clean Chuck's wounds with a moistened cloth; after that, with the same cloth, which she dipped in a washbasin, she cleaned the minor scratches that Cadoc had sustained in his face and on the arms.

Chapter 10

"We can put the building to good use," Earl Dugan said. "We can turn the upper floor into municipal chambers, and the barroom itself into a hall for council meetings or other community events. We can also use one part as a stage depot."

"Who was to think that some day Jericho would have such a beautiful town hall!" Jeremy commented.

"We must thank Macum Bersa himself for that. He did some good for the town after all, though he didn't mean to."

They were in the Sheriff's office, lounging in chairs on opposite sides of the desk, which supported Earl Dugan's legs.

"What do you intend to do with those?" Jeremy looked towards the Crusaders who were locked inside the cell and who had various parts of their bodies bandaged.

"I don't want them to stay here. Folks are liable to have a necktie party for them, taking the law in their own hands. I've asked for some federal officers to be sent from Santa Fé. I expect them to arrive soon to pick up the prisoners. After that they'll be the responsibility of the territorial judge. Maybe they'll be sentenced to die anyhow."

"And what are we going to do with the saloon girls? Are you going to permit them to stay in Jericho?" Jeremy was referring to the Paradise's female staff that had been rounded up after the gun battle.

"The town council has to decide that. I don't believe that the people of this town want any more of these activities. Bersa started all this. Now he's gone, and these harlots can go too. We'll send them back to where they came from originally."

"And Bersa?"

"He's gone, and I don't think he'll return, after the lickin' he took. We'll advise the territorial authorities and let them handle the matter. They can put out wanted posters for him. Bottom line – this is no longer within my jurisdiction."

"I just hope you're right in thinking that Bersa's gone forever," Jeremy said uneasily. "We shouldn't underestimate him."

"What are you saying, Reverend? You really believe he'd have the gall to come back here some day? Well, just let him try. We'll have the town well guarded from now on, and if he actually does return, he'll regret the day and the hour. Just you let him try…." Earl Dugan chuckled, rubbing his hands fiendishly.

The door opened, and Hutchison stepped in, tipping his hat. "Sheriff….Reverend."

"Howdy Abe," they returned the greeting, and Earl Dugan asked, "How are you getting on with the preparations for the burial?"

"We're just about done. We dug a hole big enough to hold all of them guards. It ain't gonna be comfortable for them to be together in one single place, but really, they don't deserve any better; and I sure ain't gonna hammer together a special box for each and every one of them." He laughed with contempt; then he turned solemn. "We've also dug graves for Kimball, Woodruff and Stevens – may they rest in peace – and for the Harrison girl, poor thing. For them the coffins are ready."

Earl Dugan looked to Jeremy. "Reverend, I believe your services are needed. They're waiting for us outside. Let me get Prentiss. He'll handle things around here while I'm gone."

When they stepped out in the street, there was a small cortege waiting for them, formed by buckboards and other horse-drawn vehicles that now were not gaily decorated but looked stark without the flowers. In them were the grieving townsfolk, dressed drably, and many of them with tears in their eyes. Kimball, Woodruff and Stevens, as well as Brandy, had become symbolic figures for them – symbolic of ten years of suffering and destruction under Bersa. Jeremy climbed on the carriage behind the flat wagon that bore the four coffins, and was greeted silently by familiar faces – the Doc, stiff-legged from his injury, Adams with a bandage around his head and Thompson, unharmed but somber. In the vehicle that followed were Johnny Shine and Old Man Clark -- both unnaturally grave – who were joined by the Sheriff and Hutchison. Still farther back, sitting by himself in a showy spring wagon, was Maynard Stovall. After Jeremy, the Sheriff and Hutchison had accommodated themselves, the funeral cortege proceeded up the hill towards the outskirts of town in silence.

At the cemetery there were four fresh rectangular openings in the ground, ready to receive the earthly remains of the four members of the community, besides one large trough already filled with cadavers in black suits. Having lowered the coffins from the flat wagon into the graves, the mourners formed a circle around the latter, and Jeremy did what was expected of him.

"Citizens of Jericho, friends, comrades-in-arms," he began, pulling a bible from his coat. "Before us we have four of our own – three men and one young woman – who died martyrs for a sacred cause, the noblest cause for which any human being can lay down his or her life: freedom. They died for our freedom, freedom in the name of the Lord. May their graves always be a reminder of the struggle we had to go through to achieve that freedom that we are enjoying now. Brandy Harrison, torn from the bosom of her family and thrown into a life of sin against her will, nevertheless did not fail to contribute to our struggle in the most unselfish manner …." Jeremy thought of his escape with her help. "…And the three friends whom we are putting to rest alongside of her – all of them upstanding members of the community – fought in our ranks with great courage, disregarding their own safety in favor of the town's interest. Had it not been for their dedication, we might not be standing here today free to conduct this ceremony. Let us thank them with all our hearts, and let us say a prayer for them."

They bowed their heads, and Jeremy read an appropriate passage from the Book of Psalms. Then he concluded, "Oh Lord, receive these four souls mercifully in thy house. Innocent in birth and innocent in death, they deserve the full extent of thy glory. Let us rejoice in thee, oh Lord, and let us trust in thy wisdom upon taking them away from us, as we trust in your capacity and will to liberate us from Satan. And have mercy also on these others…..," he looked towards the mass grave, "….not so innocent, the victims of their human weaknesses. Forgive them all, oh Lord. Unto thee we commend their souls as we commit their bodies to the ground; earth to earth, ashes to ashes, dust to dust."

He grasped the shovel and threw a small quantity of dirt on each of the coffins; the others followed suit – first the families of the dead, then the rest of the townsfolk; at last Hutchison's assistants completed the job. On each of the individual graves rose a small mound of red dirt, topped by a tombstone; and a bigger mound crowned the collective grave, which did not have a stone marker. Finally it was over, Jeremy thought: Bersa's last victims were interred and with them the last reminders of the perverse minister's deadly shadow.

+   +   +

When the townsfolk returned to the center of Jericho, there was no more holding them back. They celebrated for real this time, setting up food-laden tables on the square right in front of the Paradise, eating, drinking and making merry. McBride played the fiddle and everybody began to dance – adults and children – venting tensions that had built up over a long time.

But Jeremy's mind was elsewhere. Oblivious to the gaiety around him, he stole away from the crowd and headed for the Sheriff's residence. However, Earl Dugan himself noticed him and detained him.

"Where are you going, Reverend? Why aren't you enjoying yourself with the others?"

"I want to see Chuck. I'll be back in a little while."

"Now, don't you worry none about him. Sally and Helen are taking care of him. That wound of his is pretty bad – I know – but it'll heal in time. Once you've checked him, come back to the square and bring my daughter and her friend so they can have some fun too. We can have one of the ladies watch Chuck for a spell."

"All right Sheriff. I'll do as you say. I'll be back soon."

Jeremy walked on, and when he reached the Sheriff's residence, entered without ceremony, went to Dugan's bedroom and opened the door quietly. On the bed lay Chuck, his face glistening with sweat, his body covered with a blanket, which did not entirely hide the bandage around his midriff, from where Doc Brower had removed the bullet. Helen, a simple but kind-hearted girl with sandy hair and an ample figure, was sitting on a chair next to him, bending over to wipe his forehead with a damp cloth; and Sally, too, was present to help with whatever was needed.

"How is he doing?" Jeremy asked gently, stepping closer to the bed.

"He's got fever and hallucinations," answered Sally. "Doc Browser said to keep his temperature low."

"What do you think? Is Chuck going to snap out of this soon?"

"Doc Browser says he will, and that it's a good thing the bullet entered where it did – in the ribs. If it had been any lower, Chuck could easily have died. As things stand, he's been pretty lucky."

"It's not only his physical condition that I'm worried about," Jeremy said. "I'm also concerned about his mental state. What they did to Brandy was an atrocity. It was a hard blow for him."

Helen interjected, "I knew Brandy well. We went to school together. She was older than me, and I always admired her – she was so pretty and poised. Why did she have to fall into Bersa's claws? It's horrible that she had to end like this….."

Their attention turned to Chuck, who was stirring and who – as if he had heard Helen's last words – began to talk about his sister deliriously. What he said could not be clearly understood, but they seemed to be laments, then threats, perhaps directed at Bersa, and finally his sister's name, repeated passionately many times. "Brandy….. Brandy….." He had sat up straight in bed, and was clamoring and gesticulating, his pupils distended while his entire body was shaking.

Jeremy tried to hold him down. "Chuck! It's me, Chuck!" He shook him lightly and gradually saw the delirious glitter in his eyes give way to the clarity of a recovered sense of reality. "Chuck, it's me, Jeremy Cadoc. Drink this" He handed him a cup of water that had been sitting on the night table.

Chuck drank anxiously and then asked, "Have you caught him yet?"

"Bersa?"

"Him and the others that got away."

"Not yet, Chuck. There's no trace of them. It seems they left for other parts."

"What? Then I've got to go after them. We can't let them get away scot free." He rose up agitatedly, but Jeremy and Helen held him down.

"Easy, Chuck, easy. What you need is a lot of rest. If you get up with that bruised rib and the blood you lost, it'll weaken you so much that not even the Doc will be able to save you. As for Bersa, don't worry. They're gonna catch him soon. Earl Dugan already advised the authorities in Santa Fé, and there are going to be wanted posters in the whole territory, offering a reward for his capture. He and his cronies are going to hang soon – I guarantee you."

"I hope your prediction is going to come true, Reverend. They deserve to be hanged and worse. And if the authorities don't find them, I'm gonna look for them myself as soon as I'm better. And I'm gonna kill them – I swear to you – I'm gonna kill them, even if I have to look for them for the rest of my life…..I'm gonna kill them…." His voice trailed off, his eyes closed, and exhausted, he sank back into the pillows and fell into an uneasy slumber.

"Poor Chuck," Helen said softly. "I wish we could help him somehow."

Jeremy and Sally left the bedroom, treading softly so as not to wake up the injured friend, and went to Sally's room.

"Chuck will be okay. He'll recover," Jeremy said. "I'm glad you're here."

They embraced hard and passionately, Jeremy stimulated by the sensation of her forms underneath the dress, ready to repeat the unrestrained episode of the other day, but Sally stopped him.

"It's no good, Jeremy, not now and not here. We need to control ourselves."

"You're right, Sally. I'm a man of the cloth and need to remind myself of that."

When separating himself from her, he felt a light pressure on his pistol and saw Sally's hand resting on the weapon in his holster.

"What's the matter, Sally?"

"I was going to ask you if you'll go on carrying this."

"You don't like the idea?"

"No, I don't. It doesn't look good on a minister. Besides, you don't need a weapon any longer."

Jeremy thought about it for a moment. Then he said, "You're right, Sally." He took off the belt, rolled it up, and together with the revolver, put it in her hands. "You keep it for me. Lock it up well. Or better yet, throw it in the trash. I don't ever want to kill another human being again."

"I'm not going to throw it away," Sally said. "I'm going to put it there in the corner cabinet, just in case. Because some day another Bersa might arrive – the world is full of them. And if not, it'll always be a reminder of the old one and of the good fortune the Lord blessed us with in delivering us from him." She placed the roll on one of the shelves, behind some linen, and locked the cabinet.

+   +   +

Down the hall, the door opened to the room in which Chuck lay, and Helen, sitting next to the bed, saw Mrs. Hutchison come in. The undertaker's wife, she was a roly-poly matron, who exuded warmth and kindness. She directed a kind smile at Helen. "They sent me to take your place. How's the Harrison boy doing?"

"He's resting. He fell asleep after a fever attack. Doc Browser says to wipe him with this and keep him cool at all times." Helen pointed to a rag which was floating in a water bowl.

"I understand, girl. I've had to take care of quite a few injured men in my time, not to mention all them kids with measles. Sheriff Dugan wants you, Sally and Reverend Cadoc to come to the square to join in the celebration. That's why he sent me."

"Thank you, Mrs. Hutchison, but I'm going to stay here. Chuck and I have known each other for many years, and I want to take care of him. But please advise Sally and the Reverend. I think they're in the next room."

Mrs. Hutchinson, following her suggestion, knocked lightly on the next door. Jeremy pulled apart from Sally, and the latter arranged her hair. Then the stately lady entered and said, "You and the Reverend go and have some fun."

Jeremy accepted. "If Chuck has another attack, send the jail guard to look for us, please, Mrs. Hutchison."

"I'll do that, Reverend. Don't worry. Helen and I will look after him together. He'll be well taken care of. Go on now, before the celebration is over." She shooed them out of the room, and the two stepped into the street and headed for the square, walking leisurely.

"Sally, it's time we talked with your Pa," Jeremy said.

Sally blushed. "I hope you're not mad, but I mentioned it already. I was so excited."

Jeremy smiled. "And what did he say?"

"That he liked very much for us to get married and that he couldn't imagine a better son-in-law."

"That's great, Sally. When shall we set the date?

"This coming Sunday, if you like. I discussed it with my Pa."

"That's fine. Let's not wait any longer. I'm anxious to formalize things.

They continued to talk about the wedding as they walked the rest of the way to the square. When they arrived in front of the Paradise, they were received with great noise by the crowd, whose members steered them up the porch, where Earl Dugan was already waiting for them. After greeting them, the Sheriff took Jeremy aside to speak to him for a moment; then he faced the assembled and raised his hand, begging for silence.

"Here he is, Ladies and Gentlemen!" he proclaimed, once the music and voices quieted down. "Jericho's savior, the man who liberated this town from tyranny, who would not let himself be cowed by lawlessness and brute force but stood up to them fearlessly, the man to whom you owe the fact that you're able to celebrate the way you do right now – the Reverend Jeremy Cadoc!" He clapped his hands, and the crowd in the square broke into tumultuous applause, cheering and emitting enthusiastic shouts, setting off firecrackers and tossing their hats up in the air.

"We owe him a lot, folks," Earl Dugan continued. "We'll never be able to re-pay him completely, but there are a few things we *can* do for him. The town council has decided the following: that we name him permanent pastor of the church; that he be a member of the same council; that we furnish him with the appropriate means to maintain himself with dignity. What do you think? Do you all agree?"

They hooted and bellowed their approval until Earl Dugan quieted them once more. "In addition, I have an announcement. I don't know how to say this…." He put one arm around his daughter's shoulders and the other around Jeremy's. "Ladies and Gentlemen, meet the future Mrs. Cadoc as well as my future son-in-law."

There was a great surge of applause, mixed with questions regarding the wedding date.

"We're planning on having the ceremony next Sunday in our church. I myself am going to join them in my capacity as justice of the peace. Afterwards we're gonna have a big reception. Everybody's invited."

Again they applauded. Jeremy was very happy. He had achieved everything he had planned. It was his moment of triumph. He felt the impulse to make a speech himself and stepped forward, raising his hand.

"Ladies and Gentlemen," he said, the crowd falling silent. "On behalf of my bride and myself, I thank you for all you intend to do for us. I also want to thank you for your help in the fight against Bersa. It was you – the citizens of Jericho – who brought about the defeat of this evil man; I only helped organize your effort. Last I give thanks to God for protecting us and helping us, and for making sure our fight was successful….. Let us pray." He bowed his head, and the assembled followed his example. "Oh Lord, I thank you for all the benefits and privileges you bestowed on us, and I pray to you that you now help us to recover from the damages we have sustained. Help those who are injured, and grant peace to the dead. Let this town prosper and let it become a spiritual oasis in a corrupt world – a monument dedicated to you. Amen"

"Amen," they answered in chorus.

"And now, let's get on with the party," Earl Dugan said cheerfully. "McBride, make that fiddle sing….Reverend, I'll leave the honor of the first dance to you." With a wave of his hand, he invited Jeremy to take Sally down into the street.

Jeremy took her by the hand, and together they went down the few steps until stopping in the middle of an open circle formed by the people. Letting out a shout, McBride began to play, and Jeremy started to dance, for the first time in his life, imitating the style he had seen in others, embracing Sally closely, twirling and pulling her, until the animated faces around him were a blur and only the radiant countenance of the girl before him remained in focus. He was thrilled as never before, dancing his heart out.

And they all continued to celebrate well into the night.

+   +   +

They had quartered Jeremy in the Paradise for the night because it didn't seem right that he should be staying under the same roof as the bride on the eve of the wedding. And they had transferred Chuck to this location as well, for convenience and so that he could be in the company of his friend. Chuck had improved considerably in the meantime. He had gotten over the fever and looked much healthier and stronger, lying as he was in his bed, his eyes closed; his wound, though still tender, had already closed up; it looked like in a short time Chuck would be restored.

Mrs. Hutchison had been sent home, though Helen had remained, helping with Chuck's installation at the Paradise. But now she, too, was no longer needed.

"Thank you, Helen, for taking such good care of me," Chuck said. "But you look exhausted. You've been by my side for many hours . You need to get some rest."

"It's been my pleasure, Chuck. We've been friends for many years. There's nothing I wouldn't do for you."

"I appreciate that, Helen. But I'm all right. Reverend Cadoc is here, and I'll be okay."

"Yes, Helen. Don't worry about Chuck. I'll look after him."

"If you say so, Reverend. I'll go, then." Helen bent forward and gave Chuck a hug. "Be good now."

"I will, and thanks again," Chuck said, hugging her back as best as he could.

Jeremy noticed the special emotion flowing from one to the other, but he said nothing and instead glanced around the room they had been installed in – not Bersa's master bedroom but a similar one that had two beds. He didn't mind staying in this place, in spite of all the negative associations, for he felt he had triumphed over all the evil that had dwelled here. He himself was the lord of these chambers now, the knight who had conquered this fortress, and therefore its rightful owner, at least for a few hours. Not even the decadent sumptuousness of the furniture and décor around him, and of the bed on which he was sitting – all so reminiscent of Bersa – could take away from his enjoyment. If anything, he found it amusing. Soon all of it would be torn out to make way for the plainer furnishings of municipal chambers, and he didn't see any harm in savoring this bizarre bit of history, so intimately tied to his personal life.

Thinking thus, he got up from the bed, and leaving Chuck to rest, proceeded to take one last tour of Bersa's apartments. The stroll evoked bitter-sweet memories in him. Yes, it was here where Bersa had kept him a prisoner and from where Brandy had helped him escape; and it was here, in that salon, where Bersa had welcomed him the first day, offering him a drink; it was in the gigantic bedroom where Bersa had invited him to collaborate with the Crusaders, and where he had encountered the unfortunate Brandy; and then there was the S&M torture chamber, menacing in its grotesque abandonment. What a strange man Bersa was, with a singularly twisted personality and full of incalculable quirks and mad impulses; but intelligent he was, and even sophisticated in certain ways, and it was that which worried Jeremy now. They had beaten Bersa, and he had taken to his heels; and the chances were that he would never return. On the other hand, Bersa was not the kind of man who resigned himself easily to defeat. Possibly he would seek revenge. To be sure, the town was well guarded by the members of the militia that Earl Dugan had organized so that there was no reason to be worried.

Leaving Bersa's apartments, Jeremy stepped out on the gallery that overlooked the interior of the saloon, dominating the large premises from above. No longer were there any signs of the violent battle that had raged here; the place was gaily decorated with flowers and equipped with long tables, covered with white linen.

Here the wedding banquet would take place tomorrow; it was the only place big enough to accommodate all the guests – practically the whole town of Jericho. The ceremony itself would be conducted by Earl Dugan, after which Jeremy himself would hold a religious service – his first in Jericho, his first in his own church, his first performed without the help of a more experienced pastor. It would be the culminating point of his life until now, and the beginning of a new phase, a phase which would signify his maturation as a minister and as a human being.. He could already imagine the occasion, the congregation, which would be responding spontaneously – not with the artificial exultation of the day of his arrival; they would be singing, and he would be preaching his first official sermon – the words were already forming in his mind and almost sprang to his lips….but suddenly he was jarred out of his reverie.

Outside there were pounding hooves, screams and commotion. What was happening? Bersa? Electrified, Jeremy ran down the staircas, crossed the barroom and stepped out the swing door. He paused in the street in order to orient himself and saw a stream of men heading up the hill, carrying pails.

"What's the matter? Where are you going?" he asked one of the passers-by.

"There's a fire up there. Come and help."

The man left, and Jeremy followed him, joining the human current. He could see a bright reflection against the night sky which grew more intense as he advanced. It had to be one of the last houses on the way out of town. But, advancing still further in the midst of the crowd, he realized that it couldn't possibly be one of those houses – the glow was too gigantic, drowning out an ever-increasing number of stars in the sky; it probably was a much larger structure than the flat dwellings at that end of the town. Suddenly he had a low feeling in his stomach – there existed only one building of these extraordinary dimensions. He ran up the final stretch of the street, hurrying even more, and coming around the last turn, found his worst fears confirmed: it was the church. It was lighting up the countryside as bright as day – a gigantic torch that was sending ferocious flames into the firmament, shooting out flares, spraying fiery showers, to the thundering accompaniment of scorching winds.

Jeremy was stunned and for a moment could not move. Then he recovered and tried to determine what he could do in order to help. They had already formed a human chain to move water from a nearby well to the site, but it was obvious that the church could not be saved. Already hardly more than a skeleton of the building remained. Among the crowd Jeremy recognized familiar faces: Thompson, very close to the flames, pouring out bucket after bucket; Adams, Shine and old man Clark, doing what they could; Hutchison and his men, working feverishly. But he did not see Earl Dugan. As much as he scrutinized the milling throng, he could not find him, and when he asked several folks, they weren't able to give him any clue about the Sheriff. He had a strange intuition, which made him forget about the drama surrounding him and drove him to head back to town and to the Sheriff's house in long, hurried strides. On arriving, he found the door open in an alarming way; he entered, and passed through the corridor, and then to the parlor, and there another shock awaited him.

The room was turned completely upside down – the chairs and table tossed over, the curtains torn, a picture broken into pieces and diverse personal objects strewn about in a disorderly fashion. In the middle of this chaos, spread-eagled on the floor, stripped to the waist, his head dangling to the side, exposing his distended throat, traversed by a crimson cleavage from which the blood had emptied, was the man whom Jeremy had been looking for.

"Sheriff!"

Stepping closer, he noticed a sheet of paper covered with letters on top of the cadaver and picked it up. The note read:

YOU REAP WHAT YOU SOW

Bersa! There was no longer any doubt left that it had been he and his Crusaders.

"Cowards," Jeremy said under his breath. Suddenly he thought of Sally. Where was she? He called her name but did not get an answer. He picked up the oil lamp that was hanging from a beam and left the parlor in order to check the rest of the house, but he did not encounter his bride. Finally, in the hallway, he noticed something on the floor and retrieved it. It was a piece of material adorned with lace – a frayed strip violently torn from a scarf or dress. Then he recognized the design and color: they were the same as those of the dress that Sally had been wearing today. And only now did he understand the full significance of his find.

Chapter 11

Besides Sally they had taken along the four jailed Crusaders, still uncollected by the territorial authorities, and had headed for the canyons. The militia guards responsible for the security of the respective town entrance had been found with slit throats – how Bersa could have surprised them with so much ease was a mystery!

Jeremy took his Colt out of the cabinet where Sally had stashed it, and headed out at daybreak in order not to waste time, allowing the townsfolk more time to organize themselves and follow later. He had encountered the gang's tracks on the outskirts of Jericho and followed them for several hours along the mesas, crossing the mouths of several canyons without entering. Finally the trail of the eight horses rounded the last of the great sandstone protuberances and climbed up its side, winding its way through the clusters of piñones and jagged rock formations.

Jeremy got off his mount and advanced more cautiously. He did not want to attract anyone's attention as he was approaching the mesa top. Gradually the sharp line of the horizon flattened out in order to reveal, first some brush-covered hills among which the trail disappeared, and then a panoramic vision of the entire mesa plateau – a vast red tableland, pockmarked with smaller and larger depressions, etched with the deep lines of dry-washes; all of which was embellished, as if by a paintbrush, with the powder-green of the sagebrush, the darker emerald of the piñones, and in the distance, where the land rose to form another peak, the broad black stroke of a pine thicket.

If he had expected any dramatic revelation as to the whereabouts of the gang, he was disappointed. There was nothing obvious that struck the eye – no moving figures, no horses or riders, nor any sign of human presence on the plateau. However, after examining the landscape a while longer, he did seem to see something that did not belong in the natural environment, a column of grey rising up through the shimmering atmosphere. Was it the evaporating morning haze? No, it was too well-defined in its narrow outline, contrasting too neatly with the green of the pines amongst which it seemed to originate, and rose up too evenly. And when he measured the tracks of the gang with his eye, he found that it led almost in a direct line towards the column. Yes – that had to be their camp.

What would be the best way to approach it? To follow the trail from here would be dangerous; it would be preferable to abandon it and move closer to the camp laterally or from behind. Casting his eye about, he noticed a dry creek that seemed to run in a circle more or less in the manner he had imagined, first swerving away from the trail and then cutting back to the source of the smoke. He decided to take it – perhaps he would be able to surprise them.

Mounting his horse, he entered the arroyo, following this natural causeway until, after some time, he arrived at the pine thicket in accordance with his plan. He could no longer see the smoke but was still able to smell it, and dismounted in order to advance more cautiously. Soon he could catch a glimpse of a clearing in the forest, and leaving his horse behind, advanced to the edge of that open space. Ducking behind some ferns, he took inventory of the place.

It was not what he had expected. This was not an improvised camp consisting of military tents or temporary structures of some other kind. In the clearing below him there were half a dozen permanent houses – or better, huts – constructed of wood in circular form. To be sure, they were not in very good condition, sporting dilapidated roofs and crooked doors. And there was garbage strewn all over the ground – empty whiskey bottles, bones and other refuse; and in the center of the little settlement there was a larger pile of rubble, which seemed to be the remains of a wigwam: some of the supports were still standing up, sticking out sharply, partially draped with pieces of ornamented animal hide. It seemed an Indian settlement – one of those that had been built by reservation natives with government materials; and this one had also been supplied with some of civilization's other amenities, as the discarded bottles indicated. Suddenly Jeremy realized where he was; Earl Dugan had mentioned to him the existence of this place in these parts on one occasion – the village of Fallen Moon.

The surviving Indians had abandoned it after the massacre carried out by Murdoch and his men, and now the place served as a hideout for Bersa himself. Nobody would have suspected that the Crusaders were there; perhaps because of that they were so careless about the smoke that was coming out of the makeshift chimney on one of the huts. There were horses there; that was where the gang must be; that was also where Sally must be.

This was not the moment for complicated plans. Time was running short and each moment counted. Jeremy decided to advance to the hut and to enter without further ado; perhaps he would be able to surprise the gang and catch them unprepared. He was carrying his shotgun and revolver and had sufficient confidence in his shooting ability. He was about to stand up and put his plan into action, but he never got to carry it out, for suddenly he felt a blow on his skull which made his brain reverberate, obscuring the sunlight before his eyes and making him collapse. The last thing he saw before night fell around him, was the column of smoke, still billowing densely. Why were they so careless, he asked himself. But he had no time to think of an explanation.

+   +   +

"Welcome to our temporary abode, Reverend. By no means does it match the Paradise, but we'll do everything possible to make you feel comfortable."

It was Bersa's voice, and when Jeremy opened his eyes, he found himself looking in the face of the gigantic man, who was looming in the twilight before him.

"We've been expecting you, Cadoc. I knew you'd find us; you're too smart. But because of that we already had a fitting reception prepared."

It had been a trap! Jeremy scolded himself for his stupidity. But the reproaches were of no help now. He touched his sore skull, trying to find his bearings; then, with some effort, he rose to his feet to face Bersa and the other members of his gang. Present were Murdoch, Higgins and three other Crusaders – the long-haired Buckeye among them. Also present was Charysse, Bersa's new favorite mistress. They all looked rather worn-out and neglected: their hair was in oily strands, their faces stubbly, their suits dusty and battered; and the blonde girl seemed wilted, without the benefit of powder and rouge. They were in the middle of a round structure, without windows, though some light was coming through the cracks and a skylight in the roof. Underneath that skylight, which also doubled as a chimney, were some glowing embers – the remains of the fire that had produced the attention-getting smoke.

"Well now, my friend," Bersa said. "It appears you're the loser in our little game. And you lost a wedding as well." He chuckled, his belly rippling under his soiled shirt, and the others joined in.

Suddenly Jeremy remembered Sally. "What did you do with her? Where is she?" he demanded.

Bersa raised his eyebrows as if offended by his brusque tone. "Come now, Reverend. No need to be rude. We took good care of her, knowing she was your sweetheart. Gave her the royal treatment, didn't we, boys?" He turned to his companions looking for confirmation, and they gave it to him, smirking.

"Where is she?" Jeremy repeated with greater urgency and with strange forebodings. "I want to see her…. I want to see her right now!"

Bersa did not answer him immediately, relishing his suffering. Then he motioned towards a corner behind Jeremy. "She's back there. Go on, say hello to her."

Turning in the indicated direction, Jeremy tried to make out what existed in that part of the hut. When his eyes adjusted to the darkness, he could distinguisha variety of gear on the floor – saddles, blankets, rifles – but nothing else. Then he noticed a larger bulk, covered with a shawl, noticed some tangled strands of blond hair and the outlines of a human body – the body of a person squatting on the floor, forehead on knees.

"Sally!" he cried out, and in an instant was by her side, embracing her.

When he raised her face, he could see what they had done to her, even in the dark – the bruises around her cheekbones which merged with the charcoal rings under her eyes, the blood at the corners of her mouth and the burns on her neck.

"Animals," he said under his breath, and then turning towards those who were watching from the center of the hut, "Who did this?"

They did not answer him, and Jeremy straightened up, and with two strides, approached Bersa.

"Was it you – you old swine?"

"Not me," Bersa said with feigned innocence. "I don't like these type of excesses. I leave them to my buddy, Higgins, who's an expert in these things. He took care of Brandy as well, and I must say he performed his duties in an extremely responsible fashion."

Higgins bowed. "Thank you, Reverend. I do appreciate them little favors you grant me now and then, and try to do what I can…"

He was grinning, but in another instant, his amusement was shattered by the fist that hit first his face and then his stomach, making him gasp and stumble backwards. However, before he could do more damage to Higgins, Jeremy was subdued by Buckeye and another Crusader, both of whom grasped him by the arms.

Higgins had recovered his balance. He touched his nose and discovered blood, and suddenly started forward in order to throw himself at Jeremy. "Son of a bitch, I'm gonna let you have it."

But Bersa interposed himself. "Hold it, Higgins. You'll get your chance to have your fun with him. First I want to talk to him some more to clear up a few things."

"As you wish, Reverend," Higgins said, barely controlling himself.

"Well, Cadoc," Bersa went on. "you must have asked yourself how I was able to escape from the Paradise the night of the attack." He paused, and when Jeremy did not react, continued. "I'll explain it to you, so that you realize that there are still people in Jericho who love me. In fact, I feel that the whole town deep down still supports me. If you hadn't riled them up, they'd never have rebelled against me. Now they have to learn the hard way. I'm going to return and discipline them, and before you know it, they'll obey me once more…."

"Who was it?" Jeremy interrupted him.

"Pardon me?"

"Who stabbed us in the back? Who was the traitor?" Suddenly Jeremy thought of the banker and his stubborn, uncooperative attitude. "It was Stovall, wasn't it?"

Bersa evidenced surprise. "And how did you figure that out? Yes, I might as well say it, it was him. We've always had a very special relationship, and it was a stroke of luck that it fell to him to guard the back door of the Paradise. Stovall distracted the others that were with him and gave us a chance to escape."

"Miserable wretch!"

"And that wasn't all," Bersa continued with glee. "Since the day of our unfortunate departure from Jericho, Stovall remained in contact with us, informing us about what was happening in town. And last night he helped us get in."

"Coward!"

"No, Cadoc. He's a loyal follower, and once I'm established in Jericho again, I'm going to justly reward him."

"He deserves death just like you, Bersa. Let pigs die with pigs," Jeremy spat out.

Bersa laughed. "You've got your resentments, and I take that into account. That's why I don't get mad."

"I'll kill you right now," cried Jeremy, and escaping from the grip of the two Crusaders who had been holding him, flung himself at him and strangled his throat with his hands.

Bersa fought for air, coughing and moving his arms clumsily. At last the two Crusaders succeeded in pulling Jeremy away, and Bersa, supported by Charysse, recovered his breath and balance.

"Goddamn bastard!" he finally exclaimed, rubbing his neck. "I'll show you to….,," but now another unexpected incident occurred. A convulsion shook Bersa's gigantic frame; his hand reached for his chest, his mouth again gasped for air, and his face turned awesomely pallid. Murdoch and Higgins rushed to his aid, and between the two they supported him as Charysse produced a flask of medicine and administered a few drops to him. After a few moments he seemed to recover.

"How are you feeling, Macum?" Charysse asked. "You'd beter lie down. You need rest."

But the big man made a contemptuous gesture. "There's no time. We have to return to Jericho. I don't want to leave those good citizens without a leader. But first," he said, addressing Jeremy, "this son of a whore is going to pay the bill. Take him away and shoot him on the spot, and take his bride too – so that they can be together in death as in life. After all, it's their wedding day."

+   +   +

His wound had bothered him all night. It had begun to itch under the bandage, which was a sign that it was healing, but at the same time it continued to cause him pain whenever he moved. On top of it, he had heard strange clamors that had penetrated from the outside through the walls to this room, and Reverend Cadoc was gone, and he had been worried and confused. But finally, near dawn, he had sunken into a deep slumber, and now found himself opening his eyes to the bright light of day. Checking the other bed, he found that it was untouched.

The Reverend hadn't come back yet. What time was it? Midday perhaps or early afternoon. From downstairs in the barroom he heard voices. The wedding!" He suddenly remembered it. The ceremony must have taken place already, and they must be celebrating down below. Strange, though, that they hadn't woken him up -- at least, so that he could wish the newly weds well. It was important enough a matter for him to get up on his own now, and make his presence felt.

Chuck delicately peeled back the blanket, trying not to move abruptly and disturb his injury; then he swung his feet out of the bed and sat on its edge. He pulled over the chair with his clothes – he would go to the trouble of getting dressed; he wanted to look half-way decent if he had to make his entrance among the festively decked-out crowd. After he had dressed, he propped himself up into a standing position by means of a chair, and then advanced insecurely, leaning against the wall and door frame; in this way he moved out into the corridor, and from there, onto the interior gallery that overlooked the principal part of the saloon.

He did not venture ahead very far, however; after only a few steps he stopped, confused. They were not celebrating down there. There was no music, no dancing, no refreshments, no happy guests, no bride nor groom. Instead the long white tables were empty, and grouped loosely around them sat the downcast members of the town council and a few other townspeople, listening dejectedly to one of their round who was on his feet, speaking to them in urgent tones – Stovall, the banker. Staying behind a pillar, Chuck decided to wait and listen.

"….Friends, neighbors, members of the council!" Stovall was saying. "We've been discussing this matter long enough now, and you've all had your say. But none of your arguments have been able to convince me that it's advisable to do what Cadoc wants. Considering what happened here last night, it seems insane to form a possee and go after Bersa, just as it was insane for Cadoc to go after him alone this morning. Can't you people accept reality when it strikes you in the face? You may have felt invincible when you drove Bersa out of town a week ago, but you have to face up to the fact that that was a delusion – that our victory was only a quirk of fate and only momentary. We should have known even then that, in the long run, Bersa would be back, and not only that, but that he would crush us worse than before. And look what he's done now! He destroyed the church, he killed the Sheriff, he kidnapped the Sheriff's daughter; and once he arrives again, he'll ravage the rest of Jericho if he encounters any opposition at all – you can be sure of that. Do you want your homes destroyed and perhaps lose your lives – not to mention the harm that will come to your families? I say we have to make our peace with Bersa and welcome him when he returns to Jericho; only in this way can we avoid further misfortune. And…," he continued with greater intensity, "…let's no longer be persuaded by Cadoc's advice. He is a youth without experience. He may have high ideals, but we have seen that these concepts don't work in the real world….. Well, then, friends, I propose that we enter into negotiations with the Crusaders. I myself will be happy to act as middleman! What do you think?" He stopped, waiting for the reaction of his audience.

They appeared undecided, avoiding his gaze, remaining motionless in their chairs.

"We must resolve this matter as soon as possible," Stovall pressed. "Very likely Bersa will return soon…… Clark, what's your opinion?"

The aging proprietor of the livery stable took off his hat and scratched his grey-stubbled pate. "I ain't sure, Maynard. I ain't got enough energy left to take on the Crusaders, but I wouldn't want to abandon Cadoc neither…."

"What about you, Thompson?"

"I can't make up my mind neither. I've got a wife and kids, just like the rest of the folks here, and I worry about them. On the other hand, we owe a lot to that young Reverend….."

"Adams?"

"I've got my store, and don't want to lose it. But I figure we owe a debt to Earl Dugan. Are we gonna forget about him just like that? I don't know…."

"Shine?"

"I agree. We can't forget what they did to Earl, nor the fact that they kidnapped Sally. But I don't know if we're capable of overcoming the Crusaders for the second time. I'm not sure….."

"Hutchison?"

"I don't know….I ain't sure neither….."

"Doc?"

"I don't know what to say…"

"Okay," Stovall resumed his interrupted harangue. "Since none of you can make up their minds, I'll have to take the matter in hand myself. Someone here has to make a decision. It'll be for the good of the town. I propose, then, to put myself in contact with the Crusaders immediately in order to invite them to return to Jericho, with the condition that they do not harm our people or our properties. I'm going to look for them right now. I don't know where to find them…..but," he suddenly became agitated, "perhaps none of this will be necessary……"

He looked towards the street, from where came the sound of horses and human voices, a clamor that surged up to the Paradise, where it stopped. There were footsteps in the dust, then on the porch; the swing door burst open, and into the barroom stepped Macum Bersa himself, a broad grin on his unwashed face, his entourage in his wake.

"Well,well,well, Gentlemen," the big man pronounced. "There's no place like home. And what a pleasure it is for a preacher to re-join his flock. Did you miss me, Doc?" He gave Doc Browser a light smack on the cheek, which nevertheless was hard enough to make his victim's hat tilt. "And you, Thompson, how did you manage to go on without the Crusaders? Did they bring enough horses to shoe? Your business must have dropped off a mite during our absence. And you, Shine, you still have customers who want a shave? Generally the folks around here aren't too particular about their grooming. And here's my special friend, Maynard Stovall!" He gave the banker a big bearhug. What a pleasure to see you! Tell me, have you had a lot of transactions lately? Well, all right, we're here to help you, so that your establishment won't go broke. How do you like that?"

Stovall smiled amiably. "I like that a lot, Reverend."

"Relax, Gentlemen," Bersa continued. "You'll be all back in business in no time, and everything will be returning to its natural rhythm. Your old pastor is back and will take care of his sheep again. In the name of our Lord….Amen."

"Amen," two or three of those present said meekly.

"Good, very good," Bersa said with satisfaction. Then his features hardened. "But no more of your naughty little tricks. From now on behave yourselves and do what I tell you. And never again listen to some upstart like that Cadoc." He paused to observe the effect of his words on the assembled; they bore grave expressions on their faces. "To be sure, I realize that you're sorry for what happened, and I'll forgive you this time. If something similar happens in the future, I'll have to take stronger measures. Your friend, the Reverend, for example, was stubborn and wouldn't listen to me, so he had to pay the price. You can find him there on the reservation and see the consequences of his behavior. We all have to mature, and if we don't do it by means of good advice, it has to be by punishment." He cackled sarcastically. "And now, friends, we shall celebrate my return. You're all invited, no – attendance is obligatory. It would be a crime not to mark this joyous occasion in the appropriate manner. Murdoch…. Higgins….boys – bring out whatever liquor you can find. Adams – the food is your responsibility; open the locks of your storeroom… I myself will go upstairs to my suite to clean up. I'll be back in a little while. Go on, boys! Get to it!"

He climbed up the stairs, taking Charysse with him, while some of the Crusaders jumped behind the bar to bring out the bottles, and Adams, with several others, left for the store.

Chuck – as soon as Bersa's speech was over – had already begun his retreat. Limping, he passed through the luxurious rooms and down the back corridor until he found the Paradise's rear exit door. Opening it, he dove into the bright light of the afternoon. As quickly as he could, he hobbled along the backside of the Paradise, continuing along the back of the next two or three buildings until he arrived at the livery stable. There he found a horse, which he mounted with great effort. Then he rode away from the town, first at a slow pace, and then – leaving behind the last houses – at a gallop, pointing his mount towards the reservation.

Chapter 12

The dust wanted him. It beckoned him to rest his weary bones on its gentle flank and merge with it to find oblivion, and when he resisted its temptation, it fought for him like a jealous mistress, entering his lungs and weakening him, totally enveloping him and pulling him down into its arms. However, Jeremy would not allow himself to be subdued; he dragged his body forward another few feet, towards the huts from where they had brought him earlier in order to be executed. But suddenly he had to cough and retch, collapsing once more. He could feel the thumping of his heart against the ground, the pain in his loin and stomach, where Murdoch had pounded him without mercy, the vertigo in his brain, drained of oxygen. He had felt the jolt when Murdoch fired the pistol, throwing him on his back, and he could still feel the pressure now; and when he touched his chest, his hand found blood. But it hadn't been a fatal injury. The bible he carried in the inside pocket of his coat – bound in rawhide tough as steel – had prevented that. It was now in shreds, some pieces of it plastered against his skin and mixed with his flesh. The hardy volume must have cushioned and diverted the bullet sufficiently to give him a reprieve from death. Sally…..Suddenly the memory of the screams returned to his consciousness again, horrible, un-earthly shrieks – her shrieks – which had come from the main hut but to which he had not been able to respond, immobilized as he was by the rough treatment he had re-ceived from Murdoch and his companions. He must have been unconscious for several hours. The Crusaders were no longer around; there remained only he himself, the huts and a tremendous silence. Jeremy resumed his bat-tle with the dust, dragging himself forward towards the hut where Sally was. But again he collapsed, remaining stretched out on the ground in despair.

He heard hoofbeats and the footsteps of a man. Someone grasped him and turned him over.

"Reverend!"

"Chuck." His voice was a murmur.

"What happened, Reverend?"

"Help me, Chuck….."

Chuck laboriously straightened him up, support-ing him around his back, and led him to a well that was a few steps away. There he sat Jeremy down, accommodat-ing him against the rim, and brought some water. Jeremy drank eagerly.

"What happened? Tell me," Chuck repeated while examining his friend's chest injury.

Jeremy, as well as he could, related the recent events, coughing and fighting for breath from time to time: how he had reached Falling Moon's village, his confrontation with Bersa, the torture he had suffered at Murdoch's hands and the execution, and finally, the fortunate way in which he had been saved by his biblical shield. Then he passed out.

When he woke up, he felt much stronger, though when he moved, he still felt a pain in his chest. Chuck had bandaged him up with strips made from his shirt.

"You really were lucky, Reverend," he said. "You've got a flesh wound and a cracked rib, nothing more serious."

He offered Jeremy more water, and the latter drank it in big gulps, splashing his face with the rest. At last Jeremy got to his feet, controlling his pain as he did so. He took a few tentative steps; it looked like he would be able to manage.

"Let's go to the hut, Chuck," he said.

But Chuck held him back. "No, Reverend. You must not go."

Jeremy freed himself from his grasp. "I want to see what's there."

There was no stopping him. The only thing that Chuck could do was accompany him and be at his side. He himself had already gone to the hut and knew what was awaiting them.

On entering the round structure, Jeremy could not distinguish anything initially; but as soon as his eyes had adjusted to the darkness, he did notice something – a twisted strip of cloth on the ground, and following it with his gaze, a larger piece: the corner of a dress whose delicate texture was brutally crushed and soiled. His heartbeat raced, his mind was flooded with ominous presentiments. The remainder of the dress, along with its wearer, were mercifully covered with a blanket, though the girl's head was visible, dangling lifeless to the side.

"Sally!" Jeremy exclaimed. He sank down and pulled back the blanket, and seeing her half-naked body, damaged by blows, could no longer control himself. He was shaken by a silent sob.

Chuck stayed behind, allowing him to unburden himself. He was prepared to wait patiently, for he knew what it meant to lose a loved one.

After a while Jeremy grew calmer and straightened up. "Let's bury her, Chuck."

They dug a grave at the foot of a pine, and put her to rest there. Jeremy offered a brief blessing; then he said soberly. "Let's find Bersa."

It was already late in the afternoon, and they set out for Jericho, both of them mounted on Chuck's horse. On the way Chuck told Jeremy what had happened in the Paradise that day, especially with reference to Stovall's treachery, and Jeremy updated his friend about his own experiences, relating to him in particular what he had heard concerning Higgins and his abuse of Brandy. When they arrived, they already had a plan prepared to carry out justice. First they were going to see the banker.

Night was falling when, ducking into the shadows of the first houses, they entered the town.

I   +   +

Maynard Stovall rested his legs on the corner of his desk and leaned back in his favorite chair, rubbing his eyes. Then he sipped some water from a glass to wash down some medicine he had taken in order to relieve the pounding in his head. To spend the whole day boozing with Bersa was not an ideal way of passing the time, but then, he had put up with worse, and business was business. What

Bersa had said was true – his dealings had dropped off considerably after the Crusaders' departure, for, even though their deposits had remained in his bank, the lack of the activity normally generated by them had already become noticeable and had affected his profits. There were no more purchase orders for investment bonds back east, no more transports of funds, no more processing of invoices for shipments of luxury products from the fancy stores in Saint Louis – services which Stovall used to render Bersa for a handsome fee. All that was left was the handling of the townspeople's modest accounts and some very limited loans. But now things were brightening up again. Bersa was back, and with him the old profits would return. With the mere thought, Stovall's headache seemed to be getting better already, and he leaned forward to pick a cigar out of a box on the desk. He fished for a match, lit it, and taking a few satisfied puffs, let his eyes sweep around his private office, cozily illuminated by an oil lamp – his favorite place to relax.

He thought of Cadoc, that pesky character. He was gone, thank God. According to Murdoch, he had looked like one of those damned Indians after the shot that had killed him. That minister had no balls. But he sure did have a big mouth and had caused one hell of a lot of trouble in Jericho. Well, all that had been resolved now. Cadoc, at this moment, was either in heaven or hell, if such places existed, or perhaps flying about in the atmosphere transformed into some sort of spirit.

Maynard Stovall took another puff and closed his eyes with enjoyment, but then opened them again, startled. Had he seen right? No, it couldn't be – that quick shadow behind the window couldn't be the very person he was thinking about. There was nothing there now. Besides, Cadoc was dead. It had to have been Stovall's imagination. But, just to make sure, he would check personally. Taking his legs off his desk, he opened a drawer and pulled out a gun. He stepped up to the window and opened it, but there was no one outside – only a horse standing at some distance in the dark.

He gave a sigh of relief. I knew it couldn't have been him, he thought. My mind's playing tricks on me.

But then he felt the pressure of a barrel in his back and heard a voice which made his hair stand on end. "Drop your gun." Shaking with fear, he let his weapon fall on the floor. "Now face me," the voice continued. On turning around, the banker was able to confirm that in fact it was Cadoc, accompanied by Chuck Harrison.

Jeremy kept his own gun trained on the banker. "What's the matter, Stovall? You seem surprised. Don't you remember me? You're staring at me as if you were seeing a ghost."

"But….," Stovall stammered, trying to recover his senses, "…But they told us you were dead…."

"Dead, really? And who told you? Murdoch? Well, Murdoch was wrong. As you can see, I'm alive and well. How does that strike you?"

"I'm happy, Reverend. I'm extremely happy. If we had only known, we'd have sent a posse for you. But as things stood, there was no point in doing that. It would have infuriated Bersa, who, as I'm sure you know, has come back to Jericho…"

"Liar," Jeremy cut him short. "You didn't have the slightest intention to come to my aid. It was you who turned the townsfolk against me, and it was you who collaborated with Bersa. Don't deny it – Bersa himself told me …" Jeremy pressed his gun against Stovall's forehead right above the nose, pulling back the hammer… "And it was you who, in the end, was responsible for the deaths of Earl Dugan and Sally. Do you deny it?"

Stovall's face had turned ashen: his lips were quivering, his body was swaying unsteadily. "I don't deny it….I don't deny it…., he stammered. "You're right, Reverend. I did help Bersa, and now I regret it. I regret it a lot. I wish I hadn't done it. I wish I could undo it all. Forgive me, Reverend – for God's sake, forgive me."

For one brief moment Jeremy hesitated, moved by compassion despite his painful memory of Sally, whose death this man's treachery had brought about. But Stovall forced Jeremy's hand by reaching down for the gun he had dropped, and the only way Jeremy could stop him was by pulling the trigger of his own weapon. Stovall's brain splattered all over the beautiful office as the banker's body keeled over onto the carpet. "I can't forgive you, but maybe God will."

Chuck had been watching coolly and smacked his mouth, expressing satisfaction.

"Let's go to the Paradise, Chuck."

They left, charged up by the episode, and within a few minutes reached the saloon. There were no guards outside, but they could hear the Crusaders who were singing and celebrating in the interior. And through the windows they could see Bersa, sitting in the center of the premises, the blonde bomb-shell, Charysse, on his lap , his men surrounding him, red-faced and sweaty, laughing and swearing, stimulated by drink; even Murdoch himself was there bearing an expression of happiness. Also some of the townsfolk were there; they had drinks before them, but evidently were not enjoying themselves. Their grim faces indicated that they were present against their will – only to serve as laughing stocks for their cynical hosts.

"Let's try to surprise them," said Jeremy. "You stay here, I'll enter from the rear. When you hear me shooting, move in on them."

"I'm ready, Reverend."

Jeremy left Chuck and went to the back of the building. He entered through the back door, throwing himself against it with all his weight, which made his injured ribcage smart sharply. But his desire for retribution made him ignore the pain, and he pushed ahead, climbing up the stairs and passing through the back corridor and to Bersa's apartment without running into any opposition. Finally he reached the edge of the balcony that overlooked the barroom. Looking down at the unsuspecting celebrants, he planned his next move. The first bullet would be for Bersa, the second for Murdoch, and the third for the Crusader who was half-Apache, Buckeye; and the rest would be for the remaining Crusaders. Higgins, who was near the door, he would leave to Chuck. Pulling back the hammer of his Colt, Jeremy slipped out onto the balcony, and kneeling behind the banister, leveled his barrel at Bersa, who at that moment was raising his glass.

"….I'd like to propose a toast…," the enormous man was saying, trying to speak above the general din, "…….I'd like to propose a toast to….." But he was not able to say anything more.

The shot rang through the barroom like canon-fire, interrupting with one stroke all the activities in progress: the conversation, the eating, the drinking. Bersa, who had made a small, unforeseen movement to the side, was hit in the arm – not in the heart, as Jeremy had intended; at any rate , the impact of the bullet spun him around, causing him and the shrieking Charysse to tumble off the chair and roll on the floor. Jeremy's second shot, splintered the parquet very near Bersa, and when he fired again, the voluminous preacher and his mistress had already managed to find refuge behind a table, side-ended by Murdoch and Buckeye. Jeremy pumped a few more bullets over the edge of the table, but without tangible results.

Meanwhile Chuck had done his part, firing several shots through a window, killing two of the Crusaders immediately, and two others a few moments later. But Higgins – the same as Bersa, Charysse, Murdoch and Buckeye – had found protection behind a barricade of furniture.

Re-loading his Colt, Jeremy saw that the situation easily could reach a dead end, similar to what had had happened during the first attack. But this time they had the enemy in a tight trap, covering them from opposite sides. Apart from this, there were still the townspeople, crouched behind the furniture, intermingled with some remaining Crusaders.

"Adams, Thompson, Hutchison, Shine," yelled Jeremy. "Back me up…."

"Don't listen to him," Bersa barked. "Remember what happened the last time."

But suddenly Thompson – more gigantic than Bersa himself – stood up and smashed a chair over the head of one of the black-clad guards, and then Hutchison and Shine followed his example, each clubbing another Crusader, and they in turn were joined by Adams and three or four other townspeople, including Helen. The latter, along with several other young women, had been forced to be present at this, the Crusaders' homecoming banquet, in the absence of regular saloon girls. Helen now, with a chair, knocked down Charysse. All of the townsfolk, as if on cue, advanced on the only remaining members of the gang – those who were crouching with Bersa behind the table, plus Higgins, who had also taken refuge there. This lynching mob was about to descend on them, and Jeremy already saw a quick end to the battle.

Suddenly, however, the side-ended table was pushed over, and out from behind it stepped Bersa, holding Helen as if she were a shield, using the girl's body to protect his own. His pistol was pressed against the terrified girl's temple.

"Hold your fire," Bersa bellowed. "Nobody move, or I'm gonna blow her brains out…..Murdoch, Higgins, Buckeye – let's go."

He led the way, dragging Helen along, the others following him. None of those who were watching the dramatic scene made a move, but after Bersa and his group had passed through the swing door, its last member – Buckeye – suddenly turned and fired back into the saloon. Jeremy fired back killing the man instantly with a bullet in the forehead. Buckeye collapsed, his body twitching for a moment, but lifeless by the time Jeremy reached him, having run down the steps from the balcony.

Jeremy stepped over his corpse without remorse, and as he left the saloon, there in the dust of the street were Chuck and Higgins, the former on top of the latter, strangling him. Jeremy let him have his fill, also allowing the townsmen that came spilling out of the Paradise to accompany Chuck with their fists in the bloody catharsis. He himself jumped on back of one of the horses in front of the saloon in order to give chase to those who were escaping into the night.

There were only two left, not counting Charysse, who was being tied up by the townsmen. They were Bersa and Murdoch. The two thugs and their hostage, Helen, were not far ahead; he could still hear the hoof beats of their horses, and giving the spurs to his own mount, soon drew closer, until he could see their bulky outlines – Murdoch on one horse, Bersa and his hostage on another farther ahead. He wouldn't let them get away again!

Aiming his gun as steadily as he could under the circumstances, Jeremy fired, first at Murdoch, who was closest to him; but apparently he missed, for he kept on going. Then Jeremy fired another shot, and this time Murdoch's horse went down, whether hit by the bullet or stumbling, just as Murdoch's pistol began to blaze back at Jeremy, his bullet whistling past him overhead. Once on the ground, Murdoch kept on firing, taking cover behind a wagon, forcing Jeremy to jump off his own horse – spooked by the gunfire as it was – and dive behind the brickwork of a well. They exchanged a few rounds, Jeremy aiming over the top of the well, but none of the shots did any damage. Perhaps he could persuade Murdoch to come out of his nest. He waited for a pause in the firing.

"Give yourself up, Murdoch," he shouted. "There's no way out for you. The others will be here soon. They're going to lynch you."

Murdoch laughed coldly. "Don't worry about me, Cadoc. After I get rid of you, they won't be a problem. Those pansies are gonna obey me like sheep."

"Well, all right, then, get rid of me. Or are you losing your touch? You failed already once today….."

"Me losing my touch?" Murdoch let out a dry guffaw. "That's funny. I don't know why you didn't bite the dust this morning, but it wasn't because of me. How the hell did you get saved?"

"Give up, Murdoch, or you're gonna die right now."

"Go to hell!"

From Murdoch's direction came a bullet that hit the bricks next to Jeremy's face, making him bend back. Then the wagon across the street started to roll, moving towards Jeremy in reverse, pushed and steered from the other end. Jeremy fired two rounds, but they were useless; the vehicle was already scraping the side of the well, and suddenly Murdoch sprang out, guns blazing.

Jeremy, covered by the well, lunged sideways. Then he rolled out into the open as Murdoch climbed onto the rim of the well, balancing himself and gazing searchingly to the other side. Attracted by a sound, he turned towards Jeremy, but he was too slow. Jeremy's bullet struck him squarely in the chest, making him cartwheel off the well into the dust of the street, one of his guns discharging into the atmosphere. Jeremy was by his side in an instant. Murdoch was still breathing.

"Cadoc," he said with great effort and in a low voice. "Why didn't you die? Tell me, how were you saved?"

Jeremy's hand went to his own chest, touching his torn coat where the bullet had entered. "It was the bible I had on me," he said. "I guess the Lord was on my side." He was tempted to finish Murdoch off, motivated by his deep hatred for this man in view of all the evil he had done, but his conscience held him back, telling him that it would be sinful to kill a helpless human being. Murdoch himself helped him resolve his dilemma when with his last remaining energy he suddenly tried to wrestle Jeremy's gun from his hand. There was nothing left for Jeremy to do but pull the trigger, the bullet going right into Murdoch's forhead.

Murdoch's eyes remained fixed in a startled expression as a crimson star formed above them. Jeremy left him there, thus marked, and re-loading his gun, headed up the street in the direction into which Bersa had gone. Bersa and Helen could not have gotten very far. Their horse had begun to limp and had been slowing down after Jeremy had shot at it earlier. Yes, now he saw it, next to the mount he himself had been riding, a short distance away, standing in the middle of the street, just beyond the last houses of the town.

Jeremy approached the animals cautiously. Where could Bersa be? In the house he had just passed? Hardly. In that case his horse would have stayed closer to it. Besides, it was a very conspicuous dwelling, very isolated from the others. Had he gone out onto the open range, then? No, that couldn't be either. With Helen accompanying him, he couldn't have gotten farther than a hundred yards before getting stuck, becoming easy prey for his pursuers. But where could he have disappeared to? Suddenly Jeremy's eyes fell on the skeletal remains of the church, just up ahead on the side of the road, standing out forebodingly against the night sky, and he knew. Of course! It was the most logical place. It could be reached in a few hurried steps, and yet, it was not too obvious, stripped down and in shambles as it was; but Bersa, with his prisoner, would take to it, as it was a familiar site.

Suddenly he heard the breathless voice of Helen. "I got away from him, Reverend. He's in the church."

"Helen! Thank God! Are you okay?"

"I'm fine, Reverend. You go after him."

"All right. You wait here until the others arrive. They should be here soon."

"Okay, Reverend."

Relieved that she was safe and sound, and feeling greater freedom to act now, Jeremy approached the church. A strange emotion invaded him when he saw the charcoal remains of what only yesterday was a beautiful structure, an inspiring vision on the bleak range. There, to the side, was what used to be the rectory – the place that would have served him and Sally as a home. Straight ahead lay the ruins of the church itself, the outlines partially preserved: several posts were still standing and held together by a few solitary crossbeams, and the pillars of the steeple rose up above everything. In which part might Bersa be hiding? It couldn't be the vestibule – it was completely open and did not lend itself to that purpose. It had to be farther back, where a large portion of the church was still standing in order to form a murky corner. Jeremy advanced towards that part, stepping through the debris, making the ashes whirl up around him, but halfway into the main ship he stopped. It was too dangerous to continue; it could be a trap. He would talk to Bersa. Perhaps he could locate him and lure him out in some way, as he had done with Murdoch.

"Bersa!" he began, his voice ringing hollow through the night. "I know you're there. I've come for you!" He paused to listen, but he heard only the wind. So he continued, "You're the last of the Crusaders, Bersa. The others are gone. Murdoch, Higgins and all the others – they're all dead. Now it's your turn." Once more he interrupted himself, but again he heard only the whining of the wind and the creaking of the burned rafters. "You can't fool me, Bersa. I know you're there. You don't have much time left. Start saying your prayers."

"You start saying yours, Cadoc. You're more of a believer than me."

The words were accompanied by a gunshot, and Jeremy leaped behind a burned pillar. The gunfire had flashed from the altar, so that Jeremy decided to work his way in that direction, trying to approach laterally.

"Give yourself up, Bersa," Jeremy said, even though he new that Bersa would not go for this. But his conscience obliged him to go through the ritual offer extended to all cornered criminals. "You give yourself up and I promise you justice and a fair trial."

"Not a chance, Cadoc. There wouldn't be any justice for me. I'd be strung up."

"Then prepare yourself," Jeremy said, progressing on one side of the aisle. "Let's settle accounts. You'll have to pay for everything you have done right here."

Another bullet came from the altar, this time better aimed, splintering the charred wood not far from Jeremy.

"I'm not gonna pay for anything," growled Bersa. "I'm the one who's gonna make you pay, son-of-a-bitch."

"Very amusing," Jeremy retorted, and then decided to bait him. "I'll have you know that when you're gone, I'll be the new boss of Jericho. You left me a luxurious nest. I can settle in just like that…."

"I don't believe you," Bersa said, but he did not sound convinced; then he went on eagerly, "Look, Cadoc, why don't we make a deal? Like I already told you once before, between the two of us we can swing Jericho together."

"I don't like competition, Bersa." Jeremy was moving from one pillar to another, parallel to the altar now, gazing intently into the dark, expecting to catch a glimpse of Bersa at any moment. "I'm going to set myself up all on my own. There's no room for you, old man."

"Well, then, go to the devil, you bastard!"

The explosion came from behind the altar, the bullet going wild, while in response, Jeremy aimed a round of his own just above the flash. He heard a groan. Then Bersa stumbled out – a wild-haired giant, savagely outlined against the night sky, his head framed by the broken web of the burned structure. He fired several shots to keep Jeremy at bay while he made his way to the front of the altar and down the steps, intending to escape down the main aisle and out the church-entrance. Not having any other recourse, Jeremy pinned him with a single round in the middle of his immense torso, making him sprawl over the broad altar staircase. In an instant Jeremy was by his side, ready to take any further action that might be necessary, but there did not seem to be any need to do anything else. Bersa was no longer capable of resistance; Jeremy's bullet apparently had penetrated to his lung for he was vomiting blood, which made his beard glisten. But he was still alive.

"Well, Bersa," Jeremy said. "We end where we began. The day that I arrived and presented myself right here, you should have known that the game would be over. And if not then, you certainly should have realized it when we kicked you out of the Paradise."

Bersa cleared his throat. "…You're really gonna take my place, Cadoc? You're really gonna set yourself up in the Paradise?"

"Just kidding, Bersa. Everything is going to go back to the way it's supposed to be. We'll get rid of the saloon, we'll rebuild the church and the community, we'll have normal Sunday services and all the folks are going to go about their lives peacefully and without being exploited. Jericho is going to prosper, and we'll all give thanks to the Lord that you're gone."

A hopeless expression had crept into Bersa's features. The blood seeping out of his belly left no doubt that his end was near, and Jeremy was waiting for his fate to play itself out. Already the voices of the approaching townsmen could be heard, as they were directed through the debris of the burned-out church by Helen.

Suddenly Bersa reached for his heart. "My medicine," he whispered. "Give me my medicine. It's in my pocket."

A heart attack, at this late stage of the game? But despite Bersa's evilness, Jeremy did not want to deny him the last humane gesture, and following his indication, reached into the side pocket of his coat to find the flask. As he did so, Bersa used the distraction to pull from his breast a derringer – trademark back–up weapon of the Crusaders – and pointed it at him just as he was about to feed him a few drops. Both were staring at each other, Bersa holding the gun and Jeremy the flask, as the townsmen reached them – two statues sculpted immutably in the moonlight.

"Are you okay, Reverend?" Thompson's voice rang out and Jeremy snapped out of his trance.

"I'm fine," Jeremy said, tossing aside Bersa's medicine flask and taking the derringer from Bersa's limp hand, the last glimmer of life having faded from Bersa's eyes. "It's over. They're all dead. The plague is gone. Jericho is free. Jericho can live again."

Chapter 13

"Won't you reconsider, Reverend?" Chuck spoke with insistence, embracing Helen around the waist. "The people of Jericho respect you and want you to stay. They want to rebuild the church and want you to be their pastor. They trust you a great deal."

Jeremy shook his head negatively. "I've made up my mind, Chuck. I don't bear these folks any resentments. I know they're honest people, and if they failed me at the moment of Bersa's return, it was because they're human and have their responsibilities. At any rate, they made up for it at the end by helping me defeat Bersa."

"Then why, Reverend? Why must you leave?"

Jeremy smoothed out the shirt he had been folding and stashed it into a saddlebag, closing the flap. "Chuck, I can't be a preacher any more. My experiences in Jericho have changed me. Too many things have happened here – things that I can't forget, that cause me too much pain. But one thing I've learned through all of this is that I do not have the calling to be a minister. I've never dared to admit it to myself, but perhaps all that's happened here was God's way of making me face up to it."

Hearing himself pronounce these words – words which marked the end of an important phase in his life – he suddenly thought back to how it had all begun there in his home town of Tatumville, thought of his parents, who had taken him to church on Sundays with painstaking regularity, who had encouraged him from an early age on to strive for 'the calling', had made him give impromptu speeches in front of friends and neighbors, had taken him to Pastor Sampson to have him trained formally, and when he was a little older, even arranged, with the help of the same pastor, an opportunity for him to hold forth at a genuine revival meeting. And he had not disappointed them; he had learned to present the word of God – or whatever he understood of it – fervently, although he had never had any true enthusiasm for preaching and would have preferred to be roughhousing with the other boys instead of pouring over sacred print or practicing with the pastor in the stuffy rectory. And when both, his father and his mother, were struck by typhoid in an epidemic that befell the whole western part of Tennessee, he promised them before their death that he would enter the seminary in Dyersburg to become a preacher by profession, and that had brightened their last hours.

But after starting his training in the seminary, he had realized that this institution, while it was a protected oasis suitable for the development of the mind and the spirit, it also was a prison which kept him from experiencing other aspects of life. After graduating he had wanted to explore some of these other aspects, heading out west, and in fact had gotten a good taste of them here in Jericho, though in a manner different from the one he had anticipated.

New drives and leanings had been awakened in him, both beautiful and ugly – propensities that surprised him and alarmed him, but which he had the responsibility to recognize and allow to develop; only in this way could he feel complete. However, he could not give his life this new direction while remaining in Jericho, bound up as this setting was with his functioning as a minister. Under the circumstances, it was not good for him to stay. Better to experiment with his newly-found freedom in other parts, where there would be no limitations imposed on him by a pre-established image. Yes, he had to leave Jericho!

"Is anything the matter, Reverend?" Chuck penetrated his thoughts.

"No, Chuck. As I said, there's nothing left for me in Jericho, and I have to move on." He picked up the saddle bags and slung them over his shoulder. Then he glanced one more time around the room – the same room where Helen had attended to the injured Chuck. "I guess, as the new Sheriff, this will be your home from now on, Chuck, and also Helen's, as you're getting married soon."

"Yes, Reverend. The council has decided to fix up this place, as well as the jail next door. I'm going to exercise my duties in honor of Earl Dugan. I'll always keep alive his memory and that of all the others who died in the fight for our freedom."

"If I come through these parts in the future, here is where I'll find you, then."

"Of course, Reverend."

"Let's go, then."

They left the room and the home, passing through the adjacent jail, where, on a cot behind the bars, was

186

Charysse – disheveled and pallid -- beautiful in spite of her neglected appearance, tough in spite of her downfall. Taking the keys that Chuck handed him, Jeremy opened the cell and spoke to her.

"Pick up your things and come with me."

The girl eyed him suspiciously. "Where to?"

"To Santa Fe. I'm going to hand you over to the territorial authorities."

"What are they going to do with me?"

"I can't tell you, but it's bound to be better than what might happen to you here. Folks are still pretty steamed up about Bersa, and who knows what they might do before a judge arrives to process your case. So you'd better get going. It's a long haul."

"All right, all right. I'm coming." She gathered a few personal belongings and wrapped them, and throwing on a black cape which matched her riding pants and contrasted with her blond locks, stepped out of the cell, carrying the roll under her arm.

They left the jail, in front of which a group of people were waiting. Thompson, Shine, Hutchison, Doc Browser, Billy Clark, Adams – they were all there, all those whom Jeremy had gotten to know well during the past months, and many others. Adams, who once more was the official mayor, addressed Jeremy,

"Reverend, you can't go. We're counting on you. What's gonna happen to Jericho without you? What's gonna happen to this parish – to our church?"

"I don't see any great problems," Jeremy tried to appease him. "They'll send you a new minister from Dyersburg. I've already dispatched a report to the Bishop regarding the matter, tendering my resignation and requesting a replacement. The new Reverend ought to be here shortly. Meanwhile you can start rebuilding the church" He slung the saddlebags over the rump of his horse.

"But Reverend, even with a new minister we're not gonna be happy. This town has been reborn under your guidance. Now it needs you to grow. We need someone like you to lead and inspire us. I beg you again to stay here, on behalf of all the folks." Adams had spoken with deep emotion, and now others joined in his petition.

"Yes, stay, Reverend…."

"Please, we need you…"

"Don't go. We beg you…."

Jeremy raised his hand. "Thank you, friends. I appreciate your warmth, but my decision is firm. I have to say good-bye." He shook Adams' hand, Thompson's and Shine's.He was going to say good-bye to Chuck as well, but the latter insisted on accompanying him to the outskirts of town. So he gave Helen a hug and then mounted his horse while Charysse and Chuck got on theirs. "May God bless you and may there be peace in Jericho for many years to come." He saluted those remaining in military style, and they returned the salute.

"Farewell, Reverend."

He whirled the horse around, and giving it the spurs, headed it up the main street at a slow gallop, accompanied by Charysse and Chuck. For the last time he saw the familiar landmarks which had come to be an integral part of his experience as a minister in Jericho: the Paradise, still flaunting the same garish sign; the live oak, under which he had found protection the day of his arrival; the clapboard houses along the stretch where he had fought it out with Murdoch; and finally the melancholy ruins of the church – the site of Bersa's last stand. After passing it, Jeremy pulled his mount to a stop.

"This is where we part, Chuck."

Chuck was choking with emotion. "What will you be doing, Reverend? Where will you be heading?"

"First to Santa Fé, and then, who knows? I'll explore this wild country some more, and I'll be looking at it with new eyes, thanks to what I've learned here. And if I run into problems, I can always rely on this …., he pointed to the gun in his holster, "… also something I owe to Jericho."

He held out his hand, and Chuck pressed it. They looked at each other silently for a moment.

"Good-bye, Chuck. Take care."

"Take care, Reverend."

Finally they separated, Chuck remaining behind, sitting motionless on his horse, while Jeremy gave the spurs to his, animating Charysse to do the same. It was already late in the morning, and they had a long way to go.

Made in the USA
Middletown, DE
28 June 2021

43085670R00116